LEADERSHIP

LEADERSHIP

CBT AND MANIPULATION TECHNIQUES TO BECOME A LEADER

David Robert Jones

CONTENTS

CONTENTS

LEADERS BECOME GREAT, NOT BECAUSE OF THEIR POWER BUT BECAUSE OF THEIR ABILITY TO EMPOWER OTHERS.

Copyright

INTRODUCTION

Are leaders born or made? Some researchers in leadership and management have acknowledged that cognitive processes influence leadership and management behavior. However, little research literature exists pertaining to the neurological aspects of cognitive processes relating to leadership characteristics. Leadership theorists have yet to fully explore the connection of how the brain functions in relationship to behaviors of effective leaders. Evidence from the literature suggests that there appears to be neurological and experiential bases for cognitive processes related to leadership characteristics in individuals. Conducted as a qualitative design, data were initially collected through a random selection method of personal and telephone interviews with chief executives and project managers in construction firms throughout the United States. From these data, a description of effective construction project managers was formed and used to solicit names meeting the definition through letters sent to randomly selected construction firms nationwide. From these names, individuals were purposively selected to participate in brief telephone interviews. The responses were then used to verify the literature and the first set of interview responses. The findings indicated that neurological functions and early childhood experiences appear to influence leadership characteristics such that leaders are both born. and made. The results of this study provide the groundwork for future research with significant implications for connecting disciplines in leadership, psychology, neurology and others. Additionally, the findings of this and future research could influence curriculum designs in construction management programs and related disciplines.

The true task of leadership involves the ability to make change happen. Although multitudes of research has been done on what makes an effective leader, there appears to be no guaranteed consensus. Essentially outstanding leaders become a fine balance between traits, abilities, behaviors, sources of power, and aspects of the situation. These become the determining factors of the ability to influence followers and accomplish group objectives. Therefore, any member of any group, at any one time, may assume a leadership role, given any degree of innate traits and the circumstances surrounding the event. Different people who can effectively influence what the group does, how it is done and the method by which the group relates to one another could carry out various leadership functions. The most effective measure of a leader and his/her competency is the extent to which the group attains its goals.

Effective leadership begins with the fundamental ability to believe in yourself. It incorporates a maturity, conviction, and expertise that translates into a purpose and direction. It is this clarity of vision that gives great leaders the confidence to adopt the role of instilling motivation, self-esteem, and teamwork. As visionaries, they are disciplined thinkers and confidently trust their intuition. Leaders understand fully their environment and can transform situations to attain an established vision. Leaders can combine change with growth, take prudent risks, and demonstrate considerable problem solving abilities. They believe in people, are sensitive to other's needs and appreciate a person's core values. They will actively remake a challenge to yield productive outcomes by creating an organization that develops and fosters success. Although often debated, leadership traits can be learned skills that with encouragement and reinforcement can produce outstanding individuals. To understand the behavior and traits of a leader, one needs to look at their innate characteristics. Most significant are energy level, physical stamina and stress tolerance. High energy and stress tolerance help to deal with the fast pace and often chaotic events of today's business. Leadership brings unrelenting demands that require physical vitality and a high degree of emotional resilience. Second, it requires the ability to problem solve and draw out those to creatively resolve issues along the way. One needs to be flexible with ideas and open to a variety of solutions and viewpoints. The key is to "see the forest through the trees" and have the ability to effectively meander through a variety of circumstances and obstacles, but to keep focused on the vision.

Leaders also need the confidence to build selfesteem in others and still maintain a strong degree of integrity in themselves. With this comes the ability to influence an organization up, laterally and below as well as internally and externally. One must be able to gain the approval of everyone involved to make an idea reality. The ability to develop cooperative relations, to be a team player and to create an atmosphere that supports a high degree of collegiality, marks the true leader. Leadership is further challenged by the ability to motivate others, often over a long period of time, and guide others effectively. Peter Drucker stated, "Management is doing things right; leadership is doing the right things." The "right" in management terms comes from the interaction with others. Leadership is never an individual's directing, it's a cooperative effort fostered by listening, gathering a variety of opinions, considering effective strategies and effectively generating a clear vision. The literal definition of leadership is "the behavior of an individual when he is directing the activities of a group with a focus on a shared goal." It is the "process of influencing" the activities of an organized group toward goal achievement, as well as, the process of giving meaningful direction to collective efforts and achieving your objective. Although there are thousands of documented definitions of what leadership is, it essentially always incorporates the ability to influence individuals with the objective of achieving an intended goal. A leader needs to achieve tough, demanding goals that he set himself in addition to those set by an organization, and focus on surpassing both objectives. As important as flexibility contributes to this equation of leadership, it is important to sustain an entrepreneurial spirit. When commitment is reached by leadership, it means that individuals agree with the idea and will make the greatest effort to execute effectively.

You'll first learn about how your brain is connected to your life. Whenever a change occurs, your mind will be affected. You'll learn what that connection is, and how you can manage this connection to eliminate anxiety, depression, and anger. You'll next learn about self-discipline. This book will teach you how to practice it, how to control your thoughts, how self-discipline can help you, and how to use it to make better decisions. Attitude is the next big point, and you'll learn what exactly it is, how you can eliminate negative attitudes, and replace those with positive ones, as well as having the right attitude towards others. Next, you'll learn about what you want in life. This entails figuring out your goals, coming up with priorities, learning about the types of goals you can have, and planning out your goals so that you can achieve them. Next, time management will be deliberated. This will enlighten you on how to properly schedule, changing your priorities, getting what you want out of life, and avoiding wasted time.

Are you ready to improve your leadership skills?

3

What does it mean to rewire your brain?

Scientists have discovered that denying an individual the possibility to get to their 'right' limbs makes the brain more likely to find an alternative path... a rewire!

You can see that everything is still in order on the moving side (it is ready), but the signals or messages from the brain don't transfer due to the damage the stroke has caused.

I can't even imagine how exhausting this has to be for the victim, but the best part is that it has an incredible 95% Taub Centers success rate!

Why do the 'Better' Limbs tie-up?

Easy, our brains always take the EASIEST path!

I didn't say the 'most advantageous path to you', but instead the most convenient!

The easiest route for the individual suffering from a stroke is the existing routes or the strongest wiring.

As a coach, this is a great example of 'Use It,' or 'Lose It'. And this 'easy way' is not just for the stroke patients, our brains try the easiest and simplest path... always!

Could this be why we can easily write down our goals; however, achieving them is (usually) considered harder than writing them down? Why do some of us set a goal or follow a specific path and use the old patterns and habits so quickly?

What is needed?

The brain wires shut down the old roads, and power up new routes instead.

How do you go about doing that?

Well, we're going to get to that.

For instance: imagine someone sitting in a car and not being able to drive. You know it doesn't work yet, because your mind doesn't 'cord', or 'know' how to drive a car!

The brain must first learn the information, wire it deeply, and only afterwards does the brain know how to perform and send messages to various parts of the body and ask it what to do.

What about someone who set the goal of losing weight? They know that it can be achieved; they have the energy, the money, and the capability (they have proof, they likely have already a part of the wiring in place, if they have been around anyone who has lost weight). As the brain hasn't rewired itself, food is the easiest way!

What about fear? Always (I would tell most of us) do all we can to avoid things we are most afraid of, which makes sense, and first, we must deconstruct the old wiring!

The bizarre thing is that we all know that doing what you are most afraid of is a way to deconstruct the wiring of fear!

Why? Why? You're going to create the new way (new program), and you're going to rewire your own mind.

How about a career change? Mostly again, they take the easiest route... and they do that which is a simpler or more convenient thing, not because they have no capacity to do something else, but because we have not yet created a new road.

That is why many change their 'work' rather than their profession! Same shit, different wallpaper!

That is why our confidence levels are rising and dropping. We have wiring that we believe are actually not in existence. The objective is to make the path to the most confident part of you the strongest, thus creating a path to overcome all others.

You must be the dominant cable, and you must be the most comfortable.

Think deeply about it, everywhere you can see this happening...

For some people who lose weight, they can take a great leap (perhaps Gastric Bypass Surgery, for example) and take the easiest way out of their life (eat), so the brain will rewire itself.

For some people who depend on drugs and alcohol, they take the easiest path (easy access to substances) and may be living in an area that is forbidden from being used for months.

What about a fear-filled life? Fears are the only thing that can mask millions of fears. I recently worked with someone who is afraid of never being loved by another important person. How is that rewired? We can't create or ask a person to love us: can we revive fear?

What about the fear of never "dying with regret, making something of our lives?"

Essentially, is it easier to rewire the inner worries, restricting thoughts, convictions, and habits?

I have to say no; they aren't more difficult.

Whatever we want, we should note that the brain prefers the easiest way. The easiest route to change is to say, 'it's just too hard to redirect', we might not say it, it's more 'I tried to do it, but it didn't work' or 'I failed' or 'I'm just not good enough'.

So how do we create new routes? How? How?

Can you use counselling, hypnosis, advice, CBT, NLP?

Can you find someone with the same wiring as you? We all know the easiest way of overcoming depression, or phobias is doing exactly what we really fear, like the people above who had had strokes, their counsellors (the higher you agree that your cabling is wrong, the stronger it becomes, making it harder to rewire. You didn't like someone all that much, and before you know it, you dislike them with passion?) But they had no choice but to drive pain and fear through.

A feeling here... Here is a thought...

It is a case of breaking it down, piece by piece to deconstruct anything. Take one of your fears. What evidence do you have that the fear is wired?

Imagine yourself carrying out the terror that you once had.

Continue to play the picture over and over.

Only look, think, listen, be effective.

What are you doing? What are you doing? Re-conveyor. The new track models.

Were you ready to create and build a motivated life for yourself? Would you like to reboot your mind for success? Are you ready to grow in self-confidence, concentrate, and move forward? Do you need some assistance?

Let's do it! Let's do it!

Rewire Your Brain by Taking in the Good

Have you noticed that positive experiences seem fleeting rather than negative? You may take a fabulous holiday or speak brilliantly, but your mood declines the next day. On the other hand, when you make an error in public or confuse a client, you probably stress on this for much longer than that.

This normal brain bias is important from a survival point of view to the negative. Those who were relaxed and dedicated to the pleasant things of our mammalian ancestors were more likely to be eaten by predators than by those who were nervous and always looking for danger. Primates, who knew what was risky and told their young people that they were worried about the danger, had more success in passing on their genes.

The good news is that a very simple practice will rewire the mind regularly, to replace your negative bias with a positive bias. A neuropsychologist and Buddhist educator, co-author of the Brain of Buddha and writer of Hardwiring Happiness, created this method.

You might have heard the sentence "Neurons that fire together wire". This means that neural roads are frequently used to develop stronger connections. Our positive and negative experiences shape our neural habits throughout our lives.

For example, if you had trauma in your childhood, as a part of your emotional state, you probably face background anxiety. On the other hand, when you meditate every day, you will probably experience a strong area of silence in the backdrop of your emotional state.

The practice of Rick Hanson "Take into the Good" leads your brain to a basic state of enjoying the wealth available to us. New discoveries like this are great because brain scientists have discovered shortcuts that take years of treatment or coaching to make changes.

Here are the steps: Set aside 5 minutes.

Choose something that will make you happy right now. You might be loved by people who are special to you. It might be that you have a great meal scheduled for this evening or that you are paid for your work. Even if you are sick or injured, you should concentrate on your physical body's harmonious functioning.

Focus your attention for at least 20 seconds on this positive experience.

That's it! That's it! It's that straightforward. If you are like most of us, the mind wanders and resists concentrating on a positive experience. But what this 20-second period does is to allow the brain time to savor what is great from short-term memory to long-term memory and to learn from it.

Remember that there is a difference between a 20-second brief positive experience and a 20-second emphasis on savoring the outcome of the experience. That is what makes all the difference in the world that enables you to build your inner state on a positive basis. With this optimistic foundation, the resources are more fully available to you for change. You may have found this benefit already if you have a practice of appreciation.

4

How the Brain Works

The brain is one of the most important organs in the body because it coordinates the functions of other organs. Thus, it performs multiple functions that are important to your survival and also determine important character traits. The brain has several different parts that first must be taken into account.

The skull is a part of the skeleton and the hard-outer layer that protects the vital sensitive parts of the brain. It completely encloses the inner layers of the brain and links up with the spinal cord to form a protective outer layer that keeps the important organ in check.

It is important for high performers to understand exactly how the brain works because it allows them to constantly seek methods of improving themselves. The brain is responsible for different learning activities within an individual and this is an important trait for any high performer.

The cerebrum is the largest part of the brain and it is the most commonly referred part whenever people talk about the brain. Its outermost layer is covered in gray matter that is responsible for processing information. It has wrinkles and deep folds to increase the surface area over which it can process information.

The cerebrum is divided into two main parts (hemispheres) that are separated by a fissure. Both parts maintain communication with each other via a series of nerves and are responsible for various coordinating parts of the body. The opposite side of the brain usually handles one side of the body.

The hemispheres of the brain are divided into four main lobes; the frontal lobes are responsible for short term memory, thinking, problem solving, planning, movement, and organization. It is the foremost part of the brain on the hemispheres and plays a critical role in the functioning of the rest of the brain.

The parietal lobes are immediately after the frontal lobes and they are responsible for interpreting sensory information. They work closely with the nerves and they help in deciphering things such as temperature, taste as well as touch. They have an important role in the way we respond to different stimuli.

The optical lobes work closely with the eyes because they are responsible for processing images that you see and linking it with images store in the memory. This is the one part of the brain that associates all learning experiences by sight into comprehensive information that you can use.

The temporal lobes are the final ones and located deep inside the brain. Their purpose is to process information acquired from different parts of your senses such as touch, smell, and sound. The processing of this information enables you to react in a specific way depending on the information acquired.

The temporal lobes also play the critical role in storing memories in the brain. Whenever you think hard and try to remember things that happened to you way back, the temporal lobes are inaction because they store such memories deep in the head and are accessible whenever you remember.

The cerebellum is a craggy ball of tissue that can be found at the bottom of the brain directly beneath the temporal lobes. It plays the sensitive role of combining sensory information from the ears, the eyes and the muscles to help in the coordination of movement.

Directly beneath it is the brain stem that provides a connection between the brain and the spinal cord. This part of the brain is essential to important living conditions such as blood pressure, heart rate, and breathing. Whenever you have problems sleeping, doctors will also want to check this part because it is responsible for regulating the way you sleep.

There are also other important structures of the brain that are squeezed in between the lobes. They mainly consist of three parts; the hippocampus, the hypothalamus, and the thalamus. All these parts have important roles to play within the brain and coordinate the functioning of other parts of the body.

The hippocampus is responsible for the storage of memory within the appropriate of the cerebrum. It then retrieves these memories from their appropriate location whenever need be, and it plays an important role in learning because these memories help us understand different things.

The hypothalamus is responsible for controlling the state of emotions within your body. It also serves to regulate the body's temperature, something that is critical for the functioning of other important body organs. Other urges such as sleeping, and eating are also controlled from this point.

The thalamus is the point at which messages can be passed efficiently between the spinal cord and the cerebral hemispheres. This connection is very important because it allows for the transmission of crucial information that affects the functioning of the body as well as recalling distant memories from within.

The thalamus, the hypothalamus, and the hippocampus can be found on both sides of the brain. They are tucked beneath the lobes of the brain and they play an extremely important function in the general regulation of important body functions. Together, the three are called the limbic system.

The peripheral nervous system describes the combination of all nerves in the body except for those that are found within the brain and the spinal cord. The nervous system is a communication relay between the extremities of your body and the brain. For instance, if you hit your leg on a stone, pain signals travel instantly to the brain and tell the muscles to withdraw from the stone.

The Barrier between Mediocrity and Extravagant Success

You must draw a line between mediocrity and extravagant success if you truly want to understand the power of successful habit. It is essential to work in an intelligent way by aligning your objectives and long-term goals with the work you actually have to do in order to succeed.

Mediocrity in terms of you achieving your goals can be defined as the unevenness of working towards a specific goal but ailing to put in the effort required to succeed. Most people believe that just because they have a good plan, they are bound for success even without putting it into action.

It is a bad thing to think of yourself as a special person because this will serve to distract you from what you should actually be doing. Mediocrity happens almost without the individual noticing because they spend too much time praising themselves while their entire plan crumbles in the background.

Extravagant success is the direct opposite of mediocrity and this is marked by you managing to achieve all your objectives. It is necessary to understand both bounds as most people think that extravagant success can come without them working hard enough to move towards their goals.

When you start implementing high performance habits in your life, you will immediately realize that in order to distinguish between mediocrity and extravagant success, you must have a specific mentality. It is necessary to organize your thoughts in a straightforward manner so that you can handle different challenges that will come your way.

When you organize your thoughts, keep in mind that they can get random and chaotic particularly when you start thinking of extravagant success. Most people conceptualize success before working towards this goal, making their thoughts very random and unstructured.

For instance, most people start imagining themselves driving flashy cars and living in fancy houses in the expensive parts of the neighborhood. However, they should first think of the work they need to complete in order to avoid mediocrity and experience extravagant success that everybody is chasing after.

Useful thoughts are usually structured and very orderly, and most people will consequently remind themselves of the work they need to complete. When you have useful thoughts, you are able to see the challenges that face you and are blocking you from achieving total success.

In order to have useful thoughts, make sure you constantly have your schedule in your mind. This is because the completion of tasks is far more important than thinking about the flashy cars that you should be driving or the large home that everybody else desires.

Another way of distinguishing mediocrity from extravagant success when trying to implement successful routines in your life is by understanding how your thoughts react to different aspects of activities happening around you. Your reaction to external stimuli is extremely important.

Non-useful thoughts will always respond to the outside world and correlate with your five senses. You might find yourself thinking too much about external factors in your life that will have a very small impact on the success that you can achieve in the long term.

Useful thoughts, however, focus on the spiritual power within you as opposed to external factors in your life. Your own conscience should be the basis of your thoughts because you can contemplate the action you need to take and visualize what you will actually do to succeed.

When you think by relying on your conscience, you put yourself in an advantageous position because you can get creative and think outside the box. This should be the aim of every single person because it puts you in a much more stable state of mind and you can see the difference between mediocrity and extravagant success.

If you find yourself constantly bored, it is a sign that you lack inner resources. When pursuing your objectives, there is simply no room for boredom and thoughts that push you towards this direction will only contribute to you being unable to achieve your goals in a timely fashion.

You should also be wary about harboring fear and complacency because this will distract you from what you should actually be doing. Do not be afraid of taking action when the need arises as this is the only way for you to work intelligently towards achieving real success.

Useful thoughts usually result in the generation of ideas that will create positive influences in your life. When you are implementing effective practices in your life, consider your heart's desires because they will work side to side with useful thoughts to give you good ideas.

When you develop useful thoughts, you start seeing things in a realistic point of view as opposed to seeing things as they should be. For instance, if you have a lot of work to complete within a given day, it is better to see the challenge as it is and get started immediately rather than telling yourself everything is alright and that you can suspend the work for another day.

You should always strive to create the world you want, and this can be achieved by disciplining yourself and adopting the unique practices to a great effect. Hard work is the only way out for anybody who truly wants to be happy with the environment around them.

Non-useful thoughts are usually based on your own rational mind and can prevent you from seeing outside the box. Whenever you are operating from a single point of view, you miss out on important actions that you can take to improve your situation and help you with your goals.

The line between mediocrity and extravagant success, therefore, is hard work because you must acknowledge what needs to be done in order to succeed. Most people shy away from work that must be completed on time, choosing to suspend it for another time.

But this is just a way of attracting failure and acknowledging the importance of successful habits.

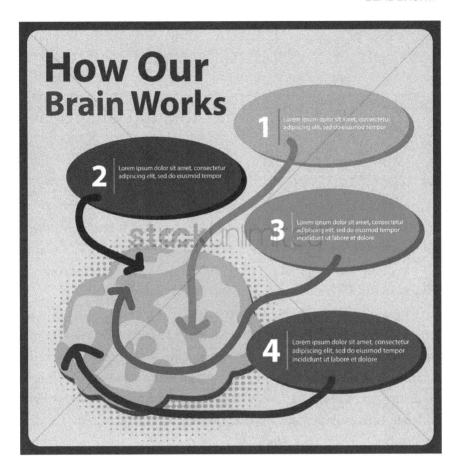

How Our Brain Works

1 — Lorem ipsum dolor sit amet, consectetur adipiscing elit, sed do eiusmod tempor

2 — Lorem ipsum dolor sit amet, consectetur adipiscing elit, sed do eiusmod tempor

3 — Lorem ipsum dolor sit amet, consectetur adipiscing elit, sed do eiusmod tempor incididunt ut labore et dolore

4 — Lorem ipsum dolor sit amet, consectetur adipiscing elit, sed do eiusmod tempor incididunt ut labore et dolore

5

Can Positive Thinking Help You?

Can positive thinking help you? Of course, it can! It has been proven so many times, in so many ways. People succeeding in spite of all odds, people doing feats that were conceived impossible, people recovering from impossible illnesses and injuries – and so many others.

You might be aware that "pet therapy" is today a scientifically accepted therapy that brings people back from depression and revives the will to live in geriatric people and terminally ill patients. Introducing an animal in the lives of people who suffer from depression/ terminal illness triggers feelings of love; this in turn activates positive thinking, which in turn pulls people out of depression. Isn't that amazing? This is the power of positive thinking.

Why?

Positive thinking has the power to make you healthier, more active, more successful and of course, most importantly happier. Therefore, positive thinking is something you need to introduce and sustain throughout your life.

Research shows that positive thinking improves the immune system, accelerates healing, improves memory, enhances your working capacity and even slows down aging. Besides, positive thinking keeps your mind open to new possibilities, which often results in discovering new paths and new options in your life.

How?

Positive thinking thrives where the mind is at rest. Hence, to ensure that you encourage positive thinking and sustain it, try one, more or all these steps:

1. Meditation – this calms your nerves and eliminates the harm done to your mind and body by stress. People who meditate regularly are known to be able to learn faster, work harder, avoid health problems, and be more empathic to others. You don't need to go through a complete how-to course on meditation to benefit from it. Just 10-15 minutes of the basic tenets will do just as well.

2. Writing – writing about positive experiences helps the mind relax and focus on the bright side. Research studies found that people who have written about positive things for just a week have experienced better moods, improved ability to focus, better memory and improved health. Science accepts that writing good things attracts positive thinking, which in turn is beneficial to both your mind and body.

3. Play - stay in touch with your inner child. You need to allow yourself to laugh and see the lighter side of things every now and then. Children fall, cry and then bounce back laughing like nothing happened. Adults need to do that more often. Playing, laughing, doing silly things improves your emotions and draws in positive thoughts.

   Make time every day for fun and play. This will help keep your inner child alive and the easier you find to laugh at a difficult situation the more positive your thinking will become.

4. Socialize – it is not for nothing that it is said, "Man is a social animal". Socializing helps relax the mind through sharing of experiences, empathizing, sharing joys and sorrows and overall

connecting with another human being. Connecting to another person normally uplifts the mind.

5. Happiness first - don't put success before happiness. Many people put conditions on their happiness such as, "Once I become the CEO, I will be happy" or "If I lose just 10 pounds, I will be okay." Don't. Do not put conditions on your happiness because once you start doing it, you never stop. Hence, you need to enjoy your life today –unconditionally. Tomorrow is never yours; what you have is today.

6. Smile a lot – try this in the mirror. Frown as hard as you can and smile. You will observe that, try as much as you want, you cannot frown and smile at the same time; and when you smile you cannot be angry. Smiling is like a therapy to the mind. When you smile, you say to yourself, "I'm okay", "I'm good", "All is well", and "I'm happy". It helps relieve tension and lightens the mood. A smile is like an "urgent call to positive thinking". A smile is also infectious! Try this next time on a complete stranger, whether they be a passer-by, the assistant at your grocery store, the bus driver on your journey home, just look them in the eye and genuinely smile. You will notice that whatever mood they may be in, they will reciprocate with a smile back to you. Share the happiness!

When?

Positive thinking will come to your help especially when you are going through a difficult phase. Positive thinking will benefit you in every situation, but it will be especially good in difficult phases such as:

   - when you are depressed, positive thinking will motivate you to look beyond the gloom;

   - when you are sick, positive thinking will boost your immune system and accelerate healing;

- when you are faced with challenges, positive thinking will get your mind to look at new solutions and opportunities;

- when you want to make new friends, positive thinking will make you more attractive and help you identify the good in others;

- when you face self-doubt and low self-esteem, positive thinking will renew belief in yourself and build your confidence;

- when you go through any grief, positive thinking will find you a way to climb out and find ways to cope.

How You Can POSITIVE Benefit From THINKING

Nurturing Positive Emotions Builds Resilience That Offers Major Short And Long Term Health Rewards

✓ Manage Stress Better

✓ Less Risk For Depression

✓ Benefit From Strong Coping Skills That Support Wellness

GET POSITIVE!!

✓ Identify Your Negative Thoughts
✓ Check Yourself Each Time Negative Thoughts Creep In And Add A Positive Spin
✓ Smile And Laugh More Often
✓ Exercise To Improve Mood/Reduce Stress
✓ Practice Stress Management
✓ Surround Yourself With Positive People
✓ Enjoy Positive Experiences
✓ Practice Positive Self Talk And Affirmation

6

Change Your Thinking and
Mostly Negative Thinking

Avoid negative people

People – who you surround yourself with – have a TREMEN-DOUS effect on your mind. It's a well-known psychological fact that your thoughts and behavior are a combination of personalities of five people you spend the most time with. These 'five people' can be real people – friends, family, coworkers... or influences – books, television, internet sites, newspapers, etc.

Your mind is very receptive. It learns fast! These influences can be very beneficial or very harmful to you. If you spend most of your time among negative people who always put you & your abilities down, you would never feel confident. If your friends always whine and complain about things, you would end being a complainer as well.

Let me share a personal experience... Some time back, I landed a nice paying job in a good company. I thought everything was great. The atmosphere was good, people were friendly, and the work profile was great. During the same period, I wanted to start an online business and was working on my blog.

My office hours, fortunately, gave me time to work on my online business, but... I did nothing. I didn't take any action despite all the free time I had. I always found some 'excuse' to delay the work.

As time passed, I started feeling bad for ignoring my heart's calling.

Soon, self-pity increased to a point where I couldn't take it anymore. I decided to figure out what was preventing me from taking action. For the next ten days, I observed my behavior very carefully and found that I had developed a crazy habit of making excuses.

I was not only avoiding my online business but also putting off office work and daily household chores.

It was unnatural for me because I never shied away from doing work. When did I start behaving like this? How did I form this habit?

I looked around and found that five of my teammates at the office were always trying to keep the workload as low as possible. They dreaded the thought of being burdened by work and were always making excuses to avoid it.

On an average day, I worked with them for the majority of my eight-hour job. My mind automatically picked up their 'excuse-making' habit.

The power of social influence is astounding.

Constant, repeated statements from surrounding people have the power to brainwash you. For example, a person who grew up in a family where people always say "money doesn't grow on trees" or "rich people are greedy" will have a very negative view of money.

Always remember, ANY kind of message that's constantly repeated to you (or around you) will enter into your thinking process. You will find yourself automatically thinking and behaving accordingly.

I did two things to reverse the damage. First, I got my seat shifted to a different place, bit away from them. Second, I started taking a huge amount of action daily to break the excuse-making habit. It was tough. It took me almost three months to get back to my normal behavior.

Be very careful when selecting people to spend time with. You will unknowingly CATCH their habits, thinking, behavior, talking & dressing style. You will become LIKE them.

Bottom-line: Reduce (or even completely eliminate) your interactions with negative, toxic people who bring you down. I honestly believe it's better to be alone than in bad company.

The good news is - it works another way around too. If you spend most of your time in the company of positive, successful people, or read their books, watch their videos, listen to their tapes... you will automatically internalize their thinking and behavior.

Positive influence doesn't need actual people themselves. It can be their books, audiobooks, videos, movies, songs... It all counts. Now you don't have an excuse to say "but I don't have resources to go and meet all those successful people".

Read their books, watch their videos...

It all counts in changing our mindset to a positive one.

Avoid instant gratification

As our society is progressing, we are constantly trying to make things easier, shorter & faster. The advancement in technology brought a new shift in our behavior. We have developed a deep fondness for quick fixes or magic pills.

Look at the commercials on TV today- "six-minute abs" or "the diet pill"

People are using drugs & alcohol to 'feel good'. In business, people are chasing 'get-rich-fast' schemes. In sports, athletes are getting caught using enhancements.

We want to feel good and successful, and we want it RIGHT NOW!

We live in an instant gratification society.

I believe there's a reason behind it. Ever since a child is born in our society, his/her mind is bombarded with instant gratification from all angles. Mom turns on the TV so kids can watch cartoons and don't annoy her with their request to play. From a very small age, we are exposed to advertisements, television, video games, fast food, and social media.

All of these are designed to make you feel good in short bursts. Once the 'good feelings' run out, you come back for more. Thus, becoming addicted to instant gratification.

Problems with instant gratification

There are several things wrong with instant gratification. To start, you lose good feelings the moment 'stimulation' ends. For example, if you are playing a video game and feel really good, just watch how it feels when you turn it off.

It's over, and you go back to feeling lousy the moment you return to the 'real world'. This fleeting nature of happiness makes you come back for more. It's like being on drugs. You want more and more and more...

Second, it distracts you from what really matters in the long term. People, who intend to lose weight, eat ice-cream because it feels good at the moment. People go and watch movies, instead of spending time together and having a meaningful conversation. People prefer to watch daily soap operas & filling their minds with drama instead of reading books. They go party when they should be working on their pending projects.

We want a short-cut to happiness and don't really want to put in the effort.

And, it never works.

I can't stress that enough.

True happiness & fulfillment come after you WORK on your heart's calling. Whenever I ignore any important work and do something meaningless (i.e. watch TV) to divert my mind, it feels really bad inside. It's like a constant, almost undetectable sadness. It makes the craving for instant gratification even stronger... which again leads to more internal pain and anxiety, which further intensifies the craving.

It's a negative cycle and something which you must break out of.

The first and the most effective way to break the instant-gratification habit is to realize that instant gratification can never make you happy. True happiness and satisfaction lie in TAKING ACTION towards your goals. When you move towards your heart's calling, you experience deep, long-lasting fulfillment.

Many people are afraid to take action. They fear being overwhelmed with work and challenges they may encounter. For them, it's like crossing a minefield.

In reality, nothing is further away from the truth.

Initially, you may resist doing your work, but I assure you... when you DO start, it will be the best feeling in the world. You will feel light.

You will feel great. You will feel that this is THE most appropriate thing you could have done at this moment.

After you finish your work today, you will have a deep sense of satisfaction. You will laugh more. You will enjoy the simple pleasures of life which you would have ignored earlier. Little things will make you happy... because you are fulfilled inside. For today, the most important thing is done. You have finished your part.

7

Believe in Yourself

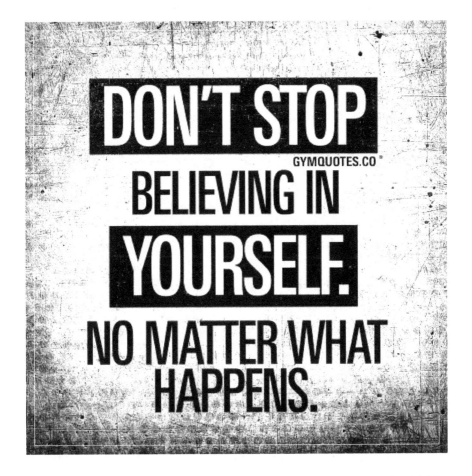

All of us in our early childhood use to dream big. We would like to be astronauts, sports figure, scientists and other sort of high achievement places. But as we grew up the society and situations start to beat us down and then we start to feel ourselves down. But what we need to do is to keep our spirit high and remain humble. As it suggests if we achieve certain position, we should not let our ego overcome our humbleness. Start off with following few steps,

Analyze what you think

There could be two ways to make your life better either surround yourself with negative people who drain your energy or the positive people who build you high and tell you nothing is impossible you can achieve whatever you want. There is a huge impact on what you read. What do you listen? This has a huge impact on your life.

The messages you receive and what you look on TV or read on internet makes your life. It is advisable to limit yourself with positive messages and ignore the negative or try to avoid negative things. This will boost your productivity and make you more efficient in all your tasks.

Do take small steps

What you really achieve is by doing smaller tasks on daily basis. It is not necessary to do neither only big thing which is neither realistic nor practical. You should set goals and you should hit that goal. Sometimes what people do is they overwhelm themselves with bigger tasks and end up doing nothing and sitting on a couch. With regularly doing small tasks you are definitely going to achieve your big tasks.

Change your mindset

The inner voice you have counts a lot. The thoughts that come to mind are not always positive there are negative voices also. Like I can't do so and so thing, I am useless. Instead tell your mind you are capable enough of doing what you like to do. The thoughts you allow yourself to believe on has a huge impact on areas of your life.

Just go for it

It is not necessary that whatever you are doing it you like it. If you are not satisfied with your current position or the task you are doing, then change them. Life is short we don't have to live with regrets later on. If you think the job that you are doing doesn't suits you switch it. Don't be late for taking right decisions just go for them.

Remain humble

When you are super successful and achieved at a point where others find you great then don't be proud remain humble. The position you have might not last forever time changes so does the position. But if you keep yourself with kindness with others even you are at a high position, they are going to respect you and be with you in any circumstances.

Believe in yourself and boost your self-confidence

A believe that you put in yourself to do anything is so strong that it can change your life. The dreams that you have are unshakable with the confidence that you put in yourself. The hope you have because of your ability. There is nothing impossible if you dare to believe that you can do it than definitely you are going to achieve it.

How to build you believe in yourself

There is always a first step. You might notice some people are extremely successful and confident because they took steps in whatever they can believe they can do best. You can also build your confidence in yourself by taking actions by first truly knowing yourself about what you are good at and what you really want to do. With series of steps attempted you will have experience which will build you believe that yes I know myself and I can do what I want to.

For instance, someone is good at writing and thinks that he could be an author than he can take some steps and can write as well. The other idea could be a fluent public speaker with giving lectures on step by step than the fear to face audience will disappear and you will realize that I can do anything. Like these you can do anything what you believe your capability is.

Don't wait for the right time to come and become lazy and doubtful about you. Rather take step now and check where you stand. With time you will excel in your tasks.

Believe that you have confidence

The thoughts that come to your mind count a lot. Eventually your thoughts become your words and your words become your action. Take care to control your thoughts. You are extraordinary in what you are. You need not affirmation from others that what you are. You have unbelievable capabilities that you even don't know.

Accept yourself as who you are. You have unique skills, talents and abilities. Incorporate this awareness in your attitude and personality.

Believe in yourself and change your life

Learn how to believe in your-self. We all are conditioned to feel less about ourselves. Get rid of such thoughts and overcome your fears and improve your self-esteem and self-confidence. Everything that you have in life is of a result that you have in yourself that it is possible.

You always have a choice

In order to believe in yourself it is necessary to believe that it is possible. Scientists used to believe that people used to respond because of the outer world but now it confirm that humans used to respond because of their past experiences.

The mind is such powerful organ that it can deliver everything you want through the power of positive expectation. Positive expectation has such positive impact on our life.

Visualization

See the things that you want and get them. By adding visualization, you will become more motivated to reach your goals and ultimately your ideal life. Start volunteer work or take active participation in meetings, take risks in your personal and professional life.

Where you see yourself in 5 years

One of the most effective ways to see what you want in future is by start being that from now. You will start taking opportunities and will be a smart worker when you already know what kind of capabilities you have and what you want in future.

Take actions toward your goals

Some people use to fail and do not accomplish their tasks that they wanted the reason is that they do have affirmations and they also visualize but they don't take actions. The reason that they don't take action is fear which is normal. Try to take small actions to overcome your fears.

8

What is CBT

Cognitive Behavioral Therapy, or CBT, is a type of psychotherapy that has proved extremely successful, so much so, that its usage has been expanded to treat additional mental health issues including many types of anxiety disorders and the fear associated with extreme phobias. Essentially, the goal of CBT is to help patients control their personal issues by first changing the thoughts that cause the issues in the first place.

CBT utilizes aspects of behavior therapy as well as cognitive therapy and posits the idea that not all behaviors can be controlled with conscious thought alone. As such, there are many different types of behaviors that are built layer upon layer over time through a mix of long-term conditioning as well as internal and external stimuli.

This, in turn, will make it easier for the CBT-trained therapist you choose to figure out the best course of action for you moving forward. Issues including depression are considered to be a mixture of harmful stimuli and an equally harmful fear avoidance response. Issues that CBT is known to positively affect include psychotic disorders, dependence, nervous tics, addiction, eating disorders, personality disorders, anxiety disorders and mood swings. While CBT isn't for everyone, it is known to present a marked improvement over some other forms of therapy including psychodynamic options. Really, when it comes down to it, whatever works best for you is the best type of therapy. Ask a mental health care professional if CBT might be right for you.

A significant part of CBT has to do with the spotting and analyzing of what are known as cognitive distortions. First popularized by a pair of scientists named Kanfer and Saslow, the idea of cognitive distortions is now used by both therapists and computer programs as a means of shining a light on the many common, yet thoroughly inaccurate beliefs that people—and machines—are prone to make on a regular basis. This includes things like jumping to negative conclusions, minimizing the impact of positives, putting too much emphasis on the negatives, and applying results from isolated incidents to a wide variety of scenarios.

Many of these distortions are based on over-generalizations of one type or another, often associated with sometime of discriminatory thought or false belief. CBT is especially useful in allowing those who follow through with treatments to become more aware and mindful of the limits their distortions place on them in an effort to minimize the effects of the same. Every person's psyche is going to be made up of a mixture of learned behaviors, if-then statements, and assumed emotions, not to mention the coping skills that were learned to force everything else to work together as best as possible. When you factor in the fact that any one of these could be warped in such a way that it has led to a negative adaptation, it becomes easier to understand the work CBT has cut out for it. Ideally, however, it will take these distortions and replace them with positive alternatives instead.

CBT assessment

The goal of CBT has never been to catalog every single issue that a particular patient is dealing with in an effort to determine what type of officially sanctioned mental health issue they are dealing with. Rather, it is much more interested in looking at the bigger picture in order to determine the true root of the problem. The goal then can either be to reevaluate how you deal with certain situations and then respond to negative thinking, or possibly change the way you naturally view different types of situations overall in hopes of mitigating trigger behaviors or negative habits.

The average cognitive behavioral assessment is made up of five different steps.

- Picking out primary behaviors
- Analyzing said behaviors
- Looking more closely at negative behaviors in an effort to determine their overall intensity, how long they last, and how frequently they occur.
- Decide on the best way to correct said behaviors
- Decide how effective the treatment is likely to be.

Stages of CBT

Therapeutic alliance: The therapists who work patients through a round of CBT treatment don't work with clients so much as they form what are known as therapeutic alliances with them. As such, instead of listening to their client's problems and making a diagnosis, the CBT therapist works with the patient to come up with solutions that make sense to both parties to deal with the problems that are presented as a normal part of the therapy. This isn't going to happen immediately, however; the first thing that is going to happen is a session where patient and therapist get to know one another in an effort to determine if they are likely to work well together.

During initial sessions, the therapist will also assess the patient's mental and physical states in order to more quickly get to the root of the current problems. The goal for the end of the first session should be for both parties to determine if they can create a positive working relationship to effectively deal with the issues in question. This alliance is a crucial part of a successful CBT experience which means that the patient needs to take a serious look at how they feel about the therapist to ensure that they are comfortable opening up to them as this is the only way that true change can occur.

If you are starting a CBT therapy session and do not feel comfortable with the therapist that you have chosen, it is important to break off the new relationship and find someone that you do feel comfortable with. CBT is all about building positive habits to replace the negative and stifling ones, and this can't be done if you can't think of you and your therapist being on the same team. If something about the situation seems as though it is not working out, don't be afraid to go back to the drawing board and try something else instead; the therapist may even be able to give you alternative suggestions.

Control your thought process: After you have successfully formed a therapeutic alliance with a therapist you are comfortable with and have determined which problems you are going to be focusing on, you will start working on numerous different ways to control your own thought processes. In order to do so, you will need to understand what causes you to think the way you do. As such, the early sessions you attend will likely include some delving into your past to determine how, if at all, it actually relates to the problems you are currently experiencing.

Individual thoughts and patterns that were created as a way of coping with things that you had to deal with in the past are known as schemas, and getting rid of the negative ones that are preventing you from reaching your full potential is crucial in maximizing your

term success. Part of this process will involve coming to terms with your preconceptions, which means analyzing how you think about certain things and exploring the reasons why this might be the case. During this stage, it is also normal for the patient to receive homework in the form of different exercises that you need to practice in order to start reliably changing negative thoughts and actions. While this portion of the treatment officially has no set length of time, an entire CBT treatment program rarely takes more than sixteen weeks to complete.

Final stage: You will be ready to enter the final stage of CBT when you feel confident that you can successfully manage your personal issues without your therapist's help. This doesn't mean that you will want to stop your treatment, however; instead, it will mean taking on the responsibility of managing your exercises on your own and keeping yourself inline when it comes to keeping up with the structure you will have recently grown accustomed to. Unlike many other types of therapy, it is entirely possible to learn to practice CBT by yourself as long as you take the required steps to get to the point where you can monitor your progress on your own.

CBT can be successfully administered in a wide variety of ways, starting with setting healthy goals, refining existing coping strategies or creating new ones, finding effective relaxation techniques, or practicing self-instruction. It can also be used in group settings just as effectively as it can be used in one-on-one scenarios. It can also be either presented directly, provided for a specific length of time, or only used briefly to help deal with a single issue. In fact, once you get to know some of the more common CBT techniques you will learn that many other self-help books are really just practicing some version of CBT. Therapists who tend to focus on this type of therapy often also expose their clients to positive stimuli as a way of creating new patterns; alternately, they may place the focus more on considering how to change the current thought process.

9

Change Your Life for the Better with CBT

Change Your Life for the Better with CBT

To live a happy, fulfilling life you will need to change your negative, un-realistic, and irrational thoughts into a positive, more realistic, and ra-tional thought pattern. To start with, you need to admit and recognize that you have irrational-negative thoughts as well as rational-positive thoughts.

Reacting with a gut reaction is not going to help the situation, and it doesn't change the problem. It simply feeds into the negative thoughts that come up. It is an irrational reaction to a rational situation. By changing your thinking processes, you can live a happier life.

When people suffer from irrational-negative thoughts, they spend the majority of their lives in an unconscious state of being. They do not re-alize these things are irrational and negative because they do not know anything else.

They think that what they feel, and think are just normal processes that everyone else also goes through. However, their thoughts and their mind are slowly killing them.

After they recognize that they are having these irrational-negative thoughts, they then have to admit to themselves exactly to what degree they are experiencing them. They also need to admit to themselves that their thoughts are irrational-negative thoughts and think about how of-ten they occur.

Are these happening once or twice a day or more often than not? Admitting the truth to yourself is the most important step to being able to change them and deal with the thoughts.

With a bit of help from your therapist and by doing homework like the ones I will list below; you can help change your thoughts. These actions will change your life for the better, so following them is key to making changes.

First, each time you start feeling depressed or anxious, take out your journal and write down the thoughts that pass through your mind.

Later, you will need to analyze all of these thoughts. Which ones are irrational-negative thoughts? How many of them are irrational-negative thoughts? Change these thoughts into rational-positive thoughts. Write down your rational-positive thoughts.

To make these changes, you will need to write them down every single day. This will help you eliminate those debilitating thoughts and change your irrational-negative thoughts to rational-positive thoughts automatically.

For a while, you will simply write those thoughts down on paper and change them into rational-positive thoughts. Eventually, over time, your ability to change them will become automatic, and this will be a shock when you do it the first time.

A few more advantages that come with the use of cognitive behavioral therapy when improving your life and living happier are listed below.

Greater Presence

Cognitive behavioral therapy based on mindfulness can help you be more present for your friends and family. Mindfulness training has been known to increase the practitioner's ability to be more attentive to those that we care about.

By using CBT, the patient can translate the need to be present into an action plan that will make it happen. For instance, the next time you are discussing something with your partner, consider bringing your undivided full attention to the conversation.

Listen intently to everything they are saying. Practice listening as if this is the first time you have ever seen this person. Focus deeply on what they are saying.

Less Anxiety

Living with anxiety can also take a toll on your partner due to the constant need for a support system they can provide. Oftentimes, those suffering from anxiety need a "safety companion," or someone that can help in times of panic disorder or agoraphobic episodes. For instance, when you have panic attacks, the other person has to rearrange their schedules to accommodate your needs.

This can place undue strain on the relationship. It can lead to resentment and irritability. With CBT, the relief of the anxiety will help the relationship improve since the anxiety is no longer controlling the schedule and damaging the relationship. Next time you are having uncontrollable anxiety, consider finding a therapist that is certified in cognitive behavioral therapy.

Improved Mood

Depression can weigh on the family of the person who suffers it. It is hard for the one suffering to be enthusiastic about life or activities, they have low or no energy, and the sex drive, among other things, decreases drastically. With cognitive behavioral therapy over a 12 to 16-week time period, patients can start to feel better.

They will gain their ability to function without the decreased energy, their sex drive will improve, their enthusiasm for life will increase, and they will find more excitement in their activities. When the individual is suffering, the whole family suffers; when they are happy, the whole family is happy. So, consider using cognitive behavioral therapy either on your own or with a trained therapist and see how well it can improve your life.

Better Sleep

Twenty-three percent of adults in America suffer from bad sleep habits. When you do not get enough time to sleep, you will display irritability, impatience, and crankiness, and your interactions with family and friends can become shaky. Insomnia has been known to turn your bedtime into stress time.

This blocks the coziness of your bed and places you in an uncomfortable state for the whole night. It can even interfere with your partner's sleep patterns. Cognitive behavioral therapy can help with insomnia in 4 to 6 sessions. It can help a person regain the ability to fall asleep as well as sleep more soundly. It also helps restore the connection between their bed instead of stress. Consider cognitive behavioral therapy for your sleep-improvement needs.

Healthier Relationship with Alcohol

Drinking too much can be unhealthy for your health and your relationships. There is a higher divorce rate among those that over-use alcohol than any other concern.

It is also tied to the violence of partners and dissatisfaction among those in a relationship with an alcohol abuser. Cognitive behavioral therapy is a great way to target those thoughts and behaviors that fuel the alcohol problem, and it helps the sufferer find a better way of coping with their alcohol use.

Oftentimes, couples' behavioral therapy is the most effective treatment. This is where both partners participate in the treatment plan. Since alcohol abuse is so severe, life-long abstinence is necessary for continued success. There are treatment programs that will work towards a modest alcohol consumption but in general, abstinence is best.

Happier Kids

When children are suffering from phobias or anxiety, it can affect the whole family. Parents will suffer along with the child because they feel the strain from the child's refusal to participate in the activity they fear. There is a saying that rings true in this case, "You are only as happy as your least happy child." With each set of parents, there is a vast difference in parenting styles. One can be lenient, and one can be strict. Since the child is causing undue stress, the symptoms can amplify the parenting styles.

This leads to conflict within the home wherein parents bicker back and forth about the proper way to care for that child, leading to resentment and anger between the two parents. Cognitive behavioral therapy along with behavioral treatments is quite useful in these childhood disorders. They can help all parties involved, not just the child. Consider trying CBT with your child, both in your own home and in a therapist's office.

Healthier Patterns of Thought

Cognitive behavioral therapy is not only used for mental health but relationships and communication as well. Since it is based on the connection between behaviors, thoughts, and feelings, to have reality-aligned thoughts means we will have more positive behaviors and feelings.

The negative-irrational thoughts that enter our minds can be detrimental to our relationships. An example could be how your spouse continues to leave their clothes in the middle of the floor when they take them off. You think, "He must think I'm his maid since he just throws his clothes on the floor. He doesn't care about me and all the things I have to do throughout the day."

In cognitive behavioral therapy, the patient is supposed to notice the thoughts that we are continuously telling ourselves. They often happen so quickly and automatically that we do not even have time to connect the story in our mind to a real situation that took place.

Once you can identify those thoughts, you can begin to change them into rational-positive thoughts. Maybe your partner throwing his clothes to the floor has no bearing on how he thinks of your services—maybe he simply is too tired and complacent to pick them up.

His preoccupation could have nothing to do with your relationship status at all. Maybe your worries are more specific to a concern you are having from some other situation, and in that situation, it is a warranted feeling.

Cognitive behavioral therapy is not a treatment plan that advocates lying to the psyche. However, it is a treatment plan that helps us edit those negative thoughts into a more accurate positive thought.

Collaborating with your family to help make this change is a great way to get everyone on board. A cognitive behavioral therapy program would include activities that are planned so that you stay on a specific path, such as placing action steps into a calendar.

The basic understanding of cognitive behavioral therapy is that you have all the control in how you think and behave. When you are faced with situations that present negative thoughts, remember that you are the one placing those thoughts into your head. So simply tell yourself, "STOP!" and rewrite your thoughts to be more positive instead of negative.

It can be quite hard to edit your thinking patterns. This is because you have conditioned yourself to believe these thoughts. So by being patient and by practicing the homework assigned by your therapist, you can begin to make true changes in your life and thought processes.

It may be uncomfortable at first but it will get easier and easier. All it needs is practice. Imagine using your non-writing hand to write a letter or using your non-dominant hand to paint your nails. These things are uncomfortable to do at first but over time, with lots of practice, you will eventually be able to do it with less discomfort. One day, it will be natural and automatic for you.

Another example of how this would work in a real-life setting can be connected to the practice of the law of attraction, which states that what you send out will come back to you.

Thus, if you are sending out negative energy, then you will receive negative energy. Imagine that you are in a stressful situation and instead of using negative-irrational thoughts, you use positive-rational thoughts; see how the energy in the environment changes.

You will, over time, start to draw in more positive thoughts and energy, and with this positive-energy shift within your life, you will be able to start living a much happier, healthier life.

10

What is Leadership?

Leadership has a different meaning for different people. It also means different things in different situations. For instance, leadership can be related to a political leader, community leader, religious leader, and leaders of varying campaign groups. With leadership being related to different things and situations, what now is the actual meaning of leadership?

What is Leadership?
Leadership is the ability of a person or group of people to guide and influence other people. It can be the ability of a team leader to influence and direct the members of his team. Leadership encompasses the act of making difficult and reliable decisions, coming up and articulating a strong vision, creating and establishing achievable goals, and avail followers with the tools and knowledge needed to achieve those set goals. In most aspects of our society today, you can find leaders. Not forgetting that they are also required to run businesses and take charge of political offices.

When you see someone motivating a group of people to work towards achieving a goal that is beneficial to everyone, you can refer to the person as a great leader. In the business setting, the leader directs the workers with strategies that work towards meeting the needs of the company. In the religious context, the leader guides the followers to work towards the growth of the organization and promote their faith/belief.

The above definition of leadership portrays the importance of leadership, which is the ability to inspire others and the preparation needed to achieve this. Leading effectively is established upon ideas that are either original or borrowed. These ideas have to be shared with others for them to be engaged and act as you the leader wants them to act.

To put this more simply, a leader is the director of the action and the inspiration that leads to an action taken. A leader possesses all the combination of leadership skills and personality that make other people inspired to follow their direction. Leaders always use the approach of restating their visions by showing the benefits their vision will be bringing to other people, and always seizing every opportunity to share the vision in an engaging and attractive way.

Importance of Leadership

The most crucial role in any organization that strives for excellence is played by a leader. Any organization without leadership is just like a ship without a captain–it will surely sink. Leaders guide the sails and make sure everything is right. Leaders are with vision, and they express this vision to a team that turns the words into actions. It is true that team members can achieve some good, but a leader is needed to bring out the best from each one of them and give a victorious solution that makes everything work.

Leaders Inspire People to Achieve A High Level of Success

Leaders are primarily referred to as one because they can inspire people to reach their goals and potentials. They help people to obtain a high level of both personal and professional success, irrespective of their fields. For instance, a Chief Executive Officer (CEO) of a company should be able to inspire his employees to use their skills and initiatives for the overall good of the business. This will increase the chances of the employees to thrive in the industry, and possibly, get offered a pay raise, promotion, and an opportunity to develop their business skills.

Leaders Set the Tone for Organizations or Businesses

For volunteers and employees to get the sense of a company's sole culture, they need to look up to the leader of the company. For instance, a CEO that overly excited about his business will unknowingly be rubbing off that excitement on his employees. On the other hand, a CEO that is always known to exude sadness and be the lazy type can only rub off inefficiency and lack of productivity on his employees.

As a leader, you should always remember that employees can habitually copy your behavior. You should know that you have a lot of responsibilities hanging on your shoulders as people look up to you.

Central leadership Brings All-Round Cooperation

Even though it is essential that each sector of a business should have its own leadership team, it is also needed that a large corporation or industry has a central leader that is highly recognizable. This leader will be in charge of ensuring that the sub-leaders and teams from different sectors of their business are all on the same page. Just like in the world of politics, despite each district or state have their governors, it is still important that the country has a president. It helps with the successful transmission of information and strategies needed to achieve their goals.

Leaders Choose the Right People for the Right Jobs

Leaders in different fields can easily recognize people with high potentials. When they want to set up a team to contribute to achieving a goal, a great leader will know how to select people that are well suited for the team. A great leader knows and recognizes greatness when he sees one.

A great advantage that comes with companies hiring leaders that are capable of managing and promoting the right employees is that their business will flourish because they have placed the right individuals in the right places. Another advantage that comes with a leader who successfully puts individuals in their proper positions is that they can trust those people to handle hard and challenging tasks.

Leaders are Spokespeople for Organizations and Businesses

Leaders always portray a good image and are always the best choice as a spokesperson for organizations and businesses. Leaders have the responsibility of making sure that the public has a positive image of his goal and business.

Preparing Yourself for Leadership Roles

Just like the popular saying, "luck is what happens when preparation meets opportunity", the responsibility of a leader is to help the people and organization they serve prosper and grow. A successful leader has the ability to create and maintain the momentum that is enough to make sure that competitors don't pass them by. Leaders are required to prepare for the future, even as they stay on point with what is happening in the present.

With the constant distraction that comes with our everyday life, it becomes almost impossible for leaders to prepare for the future while staying on point with the present. However, with solid preparation, this nearly impossible feat becomes very probable. So, what is the step to take?

Maybe you recently got promoted to a leading position in your company, and you are extra thrilled. All the excellent benefits that come with the leadership position and the nice bump in your pay shows that your hard work has finally paid off. This gives you all the reason to be thrilled, and yes, you should! You totally deserve all that is coming to you.

Get Good Training

Before taking up this new responsibility, you need to get the proper training that will help you prepare for the duties you have as a leader. This training involves reading books related to leadership, researching online and watching online seminars on what it takes to be a good leader, and of course, practicing.

Get A Mentor

A mentor can be a friend, colleague, or a family member, just anybody you are familiar with that is already a leader in their respective fields. It is always good to have someone that you can easily talk to, ask for advice, and counsel you when you need one. Advice that comes from someone who is already a leader will get you prepared for any hitches along the way. If you are struggling to find a way and you can't get from your circle, there are mentor programs you can sign up for, and from there, you will be getting the perfect mentor for you.

Set the Example

You got the leadership role, or you are seen as a leader because you possess something that people admire. Since you know this, use it to set an example in your leadership environment. The way you behave towards people, your work ethics, and your attitude will be what your followers will learn from and expect of themselves.

Plan with Your Team/Followers

Always start with the right foot with your team members or followers. This will make you carry out your leadership responsibilities smoothly and efficiently. You can begin by having introductory meetings and get to know each other while addressing the goals you want to achieve together. This act alone can open up the communication line from the beginning, and also a way of getting everyone on the same page.

Don't forget to come well prepared with some questions that you will need to ask your team members or followers. These questions should be related to your goals and expectations, and make sure they all get a chance to ask questions too.

Improve Your Problem-Solving Approach

The demands of the world today require leaders to evolve, and this evolution isn't possible without preparing for it. As a leader, you should always invest in your skillsets and abilities. This will give you a better approach to problem-solving, and in fact, avoid unnecessary problems.

Instead of using your leadership authority to organize long and exhausting meetings with team members to do the job for you, be a better decision-maker, and set things working. Great leaders are those who learn to use their strengths better and solve problems in the most efficient and proactive way. Time is always lost when problems arise, but as a great leader, preparation will help to save you lots of time and of course, money. So, prepare!

Learn to Listen Carefully

Listening carefully will help you to prepare much better for your leadership role. A major trait of a bad leader is the lack of paying attention. I am always in awe when I see leaders that strive to do better and remain the leader that people need but like to listen to themselves and not to the people they serve. What now is the essence of leadership? If you can't listen, then you definitely cannot lead.

As a good leader, listening to your followers will allow you to prepare more and solve problems that you otherwise couldn't have when you choose to listen to just yourself. Listening will also help you set a more positive tone when you are addressing the people you need. This contributes significantly to the progress of your goal.

Allow Failure to Guide You Rightly

The fact that you failed at something with the initial trial doesn't mean you are a failure or a bad leader. Always allow failure to guide you in the right way. If you fail at something and you know why it didn't work out in the first place, you can now prepare better to avoid a repeat of it in the future. As a good leader, failure should be your guide to success that triggers you to become more careful in your general approach to better preparation. We know preparation doesn't guarantee you success but also know that lack of preparation will increase your tendency to fail.

11

What You Need to Become A Leader?

Without much ado, the answer to the question is this: learning. It is said that leadership is an acquired trait. Some are born with a seemingly fluent skill in persuasion, but the rest of the leadership skills are learned in action. So what steps can you take? And what is it exactly that you're supposed to learn?

Learn how to communicate effectively

Communication is important in every setting that we involve ourselves in. At work, communication is something that bridges the gap between performance and goal attainment, so avoid these pitfalls: talking down on people lest they'll feel belittled, asking close-ended questions lest they won't get creative using excessive authority lest they'll grow fearful, and promoting a culture of unanimity lest they'll become dependent.

In contrast, you'll be able to communicate more effectively when you exercise active listening to put value on every individual's idea, when you display gratitude for their openness and their contributions, when you provide constructive feedback to recognize the different aspects of their performance, when you don't focus too much on your authority and treat employees as your partners, and when you avoid that black and white attitude of "I'm right; you're wrong."

Learn how to be everybody's friend

Displaying enthusiasm at work is contagious, and people expect that the source of such is their leader. But merely showing off an excited demeanor is not enough. In fact, there are leaders who are aloof to the point of avoiding employee interaction, who are intolerant to the point of not allowing mistakes to happen, who are unfair to the point of limiting growth opportunities for some people, and who are selfish to the point of putting their gains before everyone else's.

To get past the risk of spurning avoidance in the workplace, be friendly by respecting each of your employees and by acknowledging their ideas, be understanding by acknowledging that everyone makes mistakes and that there's room for improvement, be fair by providing equal opportunities for sharing and growth for all of your employees, and be a person of integrity by tying your goals with the goals of your employees.

Learn to inspire everyone

It seems hard to inspire everyone to work towards a common goal. However, that's only on a perception basis. This means that if you think that you group won't be able to hit the goal; you'll be prone to displaying behaviors that will not motivate them. So, avoid these pitfalls: don't be too narrow when it comes to goal discussions, don't be too strict about hitting the goal and nothing else, don't be too biased to the point of stifling the group to pursue your goals, and don't be too distant to discourage open communication.

Instead of being a source of de-motivation, become the beacon of inspiration by becoming the ultimate support that your group needs, by becoming the guide that they need when it comes to reorienting them towards your goals, by becoming a source of encouragement by appreciating employee milestones and extra efforts, by becoming mediator when it comes to group disagreements over goal attainment, and by becoming a participative member in discussions, and by considering everyone else's opinions.

Learn who your people are

This is not something literal, and it gets quite a difficult thing to do if you're leading a group of a hundred individuals. But don't let that stop you. Don't be the kind of leader who refuses to interact with different employees in different levels, don't be the kind of leader who doesn't even recognize his employees, and will only do so if you see their IDs, and don't be the kind of leader who stays on his desk all day – totally absent in the view of employees.

To learn who your people are, be a leader who interacts with everyone. There mere gesture of greeting people in the elevator proves to be effective in keeping members motivated. If possible, seek to remember the names of the people in your organization even if you can only go as far as your middle managers. In effect, get to know each of your member's skills, qualities, and characteristics. As an offshoot of your doing so here, you'll be able to learn the next one on our list.

Learn how to treat others as individuals

There are leaders who consider their people are a means to an end. They're using other people to accomplish the things they themselves cannot do. And because that's the case, their workplace is expected to be characterized by people-orienteers. Sadly, it's not the case for leaders who disregard each person's expectations from the company, who discourages creative expression of ideas and work methods, who withdraw rewards (even through compliments), and who refuse to delegate because of lack of trust.

By acting the opposite, you'll learn how to value each individual within your team or your organization. How? Start by acknowledging that each person in the company or the team has a set of expectations in the same way as you have your expectations from them. Be creative as you introduce new ways in job performance to ease the boredom caused by repetitive work. Introduce incentives in order to recognize each individual's contribution to the team or organization. And finally, learn to delegate trust in order to make each group member proud of having contributed to the team or the organization's accomplishments.

Learn how to get things done

Some leaders think that because they have subordinates working for them, they can sit around and wait for work to be done. While delegation of work is a part of an organization, an effective leader is someone who does not sit around and wait, who withholds information and is selfish on knowledge and skills-sharing, who is proud enough to seek for advice, who is indecisive, and who particularly turns down tasks that are out of this scope.

In order to become a good leader, you should learn how to: take initiative by becoming a model in assuming tasks that are yet to be completed, share your knowledge and skills in order to help people who have difficulties, ask for advice in order to foster goal accomplishment and involvement among your team members, be decisive, enthusiastic, and energetic in order to help get things done, and saying "no" in a polite manner when you already have enough tasks in your hands.

Learn how to solve problems methodically

Being methodical means utilizing a step-by-step approach to problem-solving. It will also help you demonstrate your ability to arrive at effective decisions that solves the problem, helps your team, and tides your organization through in order to move forward. So what should you learn?

First, you need to identify the problem in the simplest and clearest manner possible. Second, you need to gather enough information about the problem. Third, you need to explore solutions. Fourth, you need to evaluate solutions. Fifth, you need to plan for the implementation of that solution, and sixth, you need to do follow-up in order to measure the effectiveness of that solution.

Take note that the methods enumerated above may or may not involve your team or your employees. However, in light of shared responsibility over the company, and in light with the knowledge possessed by your employees (some of which you may not know), getting them involved makes problem-solving a collaborative effort.

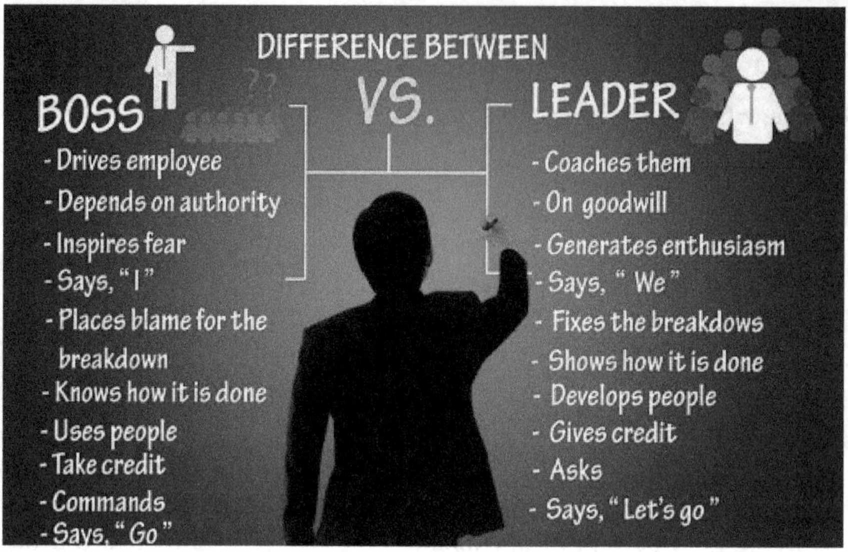
DIFFERENCE BETWEEN
BOSS
VS.
LEADER
- Drives employee
- Depends on authority
- Inspires fear
- Says, "I"
- Places blame for the breakdown
- Knows how it is done
- Uses people
- Take credit
- Commands
- Says, "Go"
- Coaches them
- On goodwill
- Generates enthusiasm
- Says, "We"
- Fixes the breakdows
- Shows how it is done
- Develops people
- Gives credit
- Asks
- Says, "Let's go"

12

Introduction to Manipulation Techniques

Knowing how to use some of these mind manipulation techniques make it much easier to make money if you work in the corporate world. With the knowledge, you are now equipped with armor to use against anyone or any institution who would intend to manipulate you for their nefarious purposes, and you are able to do the same should the time or opportunity necessitates it.

Lying, is perhaps the simplest tactic mental manipulators like to use on their prey. The simple reason is that lying is fairly easy to accomplish and does not require much skill. Truthfully their real reason for lying tends to be to hide information that would damage them or become a barrier to their goals. Because if they did something bad. Well, they're not going to want you to know about it. As while manipulators love to be charming. The thing they love above all else is maintaining appearances. So, if they can keep the appearance that they are a good person through deceit then they most certainly will. We encounter liars every day in our life but, often, fail to realize they are telling us falsehoods. Detecting a liar can be difficult, as some people have mastered the craft of spewing falsehoods, so you're not going to be looking for overt signs like nervousness, scratching their nose, etc.

You want to look for patterns of untruthful behavior that you can notice and from there, you're able to slowly build up this pattern as a log in your mind, use that to your advantage. Sadly, the truth is that you have a very high likelihood of detecting a liar in a romantic relationship than you do say the nine to five workplaces.

This is because during a romantic relationship emotion is high, therefore this places the emotional stakes higher. This, in turn, means that someone who would do something that crosses these emotional stakes is willing to do whatever required to not get caught. A liar in a relationship will probably take the form of a partner who is never home but always has some elaborate excuse for why they're absent. Also, they may try to quickly divert the conversation from the matter at hand when asked where or what they're doing. Defusing a liar through thought is easy enough, but you must be persistent and firm in your belief of the truth.

Do not falter the manipulator will try and get you to become convinced that it is, in fact, you who is wrong and not them, that your version of the truth is the real lie. Remember though if someone is innocent, they will not protest their innocence and will trust you. Simply put, think of the old saying that if you have nothing to hide, then you have nothing to fear.

Tying well into lying as a manipulation tactic, some people will spin the truth to make themselves look like the victim or to allow blame to be placed on you. This kind of manipulation tends to just be called playing the victim and spin.

Most of us commonly associate the idea of spinning the truth with news and politics. But the truth is cover manipulators will do that whenever they can. Take the example I used earlier of the partner who is always absent and always seems to have a convenient explanation for them not being present. At times when confronted with this information, they will try and pin it on you by claiming you must be insecure in the relationship and how it has to be you who is jealous since you're so suspicious of them. This covert manipulation tactic works by preying on our own emotions and getting us to question them. Getting us to look at our feelings and actions with distrust allows the manipulator to convince us that we must be the crazy ones, we must be the manipulators. In simple terms spinning the truth works by trying to downplay whatever someone is being accused of in hopes that you will believe and trust them.

Flattery will Get You Everywhere

Moving on from lying and deceit I would like to discuss one of the more effective methods of manipulation and that is flattery. Flattery is an idea we think of when the thought of relationships come to mind. The husband and wife out to dinner joyfully juking and jiving with each other. Or someone at a bar trying to pick up a girl. On the surface that is technically flattery as in its simplest terms, flattery just defines a behavior where someone goes out of their way to give platitudes to you regardless if their truthful or not. Because of how flattery can make us feel good about ourselves, it can be challenging to view it as something manipulative or bad. And the strange truth is that flattery or outright being a kiss-up is not always a bad thing if you want to get ahead in something. As mentioned, prior this is especially true if you are trying to woo a girl.

To be honest flattery in its milder form is one of the integral parts of our whole courting process as humans. Flattery used well in the workforce, for example, can be extremely advantageous for the person doing it. As it allows them to try and endear themselves to their boss or other co-workers. In doing this they will gain those individuals' trust allowing them more upward movement within the company.

The issue with flattery is that it can be used to create relationships on false pretenses, i.e. it lures someone into a false sense of security about how someone views them. Trust like this that is easily generated is always something you should be cautious about. For example, you start dating a man and he is overly flirtatious and goes seemingly too far to make you feel good then perhaps consider that maybe his intentions are not quite pure. The line between flattery and genuine true compliments lies first in you knowing yourself and your self-worth. If you are a strong confident person than you will know if someone is trying to compliment you in a way that seems to both try too hard and also be untrue.

So, remember generally flattery is not always a bad thing but it can be a segue for someone into getting you to give them a false sense of trust which is not always the best. Remembering this and what kind of behavior to look for will help you avoid being a victim of a manipulator in the future. As the line between simple flattery to be friendly and flattery for malice has a fine line, just as anything does.

Remember – Manipulation isn't Necessarily Bad

As I mentioned earlier, not all manipulation has to be used for bad purposes. Some forms of manipulation we encounter regularly such as advertising and mass media. It can be used for good, so much so that they can make someone a profit. Or they can be used in the corporate world to climb up the ladder of hierarchy. In simple terms at times, it can be required that you grease some palms and perhaps act a certain way to get ahead.

Using manipulation techniques such as bending the truth or flattery may be required here to give you an advantage over the competition. In this case, it could be argued that it can be morally permitted due to the honest fact that if you don't try to push your way into these positions someone else will. At this point you are only playing the game everyone else is playing so by going out of your way to being friendly to your boss or bending the truth in how you present your accomplishments. Yes, you are using manipulation by giving your boss the impression an assignment you just completed may be better than it really might be.

Is that form of manipulation so bad? All you are doing is simply leveling the playing field. This type of behavior is less manipulation and more in line with the idea of being persuasive or charismatic.

The difference here is you are using charm and ingratiation to convince someone further toward your line of thinking regardless of what that may be. It is still them making the decision in the end, all your doing is guiding and influencing them. This is far different from coercion where you are using subtle threats and fear to get what you want. An example of this type of coercion would be lying to your boss about the performance of another coworker to put them down and allow you to get a position that they currently hold.

Now that you understand manipulation from a moral aspect let me explain how you can use it yourself. I am sure we have all been at home watching the television when a flashy add with cool music comes on and it catches our attention. But did you ever stop to realize that those ads are designed purposely like that to draw and suck you in? Pay attention next time you walk down the supermarket at how so many different items have such colorful and unique packaging, it's all done on purpose to draw you in and make the item you may or may not purchase all the more enticing.

13

How to have a positive outlook
on life

Negative emotions can drag you into a bottomless hole. It is, therefore, important that you do not get trapped by practicing letting in the light. To do this, you can learn to see the bright side, stay positive, and avoid negativity in your life. You will also need to follow steps that will allow you to become a better person.

See the bright side

Smile more. When you smile, your brain triggers neural messages that make you feel optimistic Let your face cheer up when you feel depressed. It really works.

What do you get as a bonus? When you smile, you send positive messages around you, which puts those around you in a good mood. Everybody wins!

You will not feel better when you complain about your bad mood or because you feel depressed. Train yourself to smile (even if you have to force yourself), and it will become second nature.

Make small vocabulary changes. Some words you say unintentionally can easily make you depressed Using positive vocabulary has been shown to improve mood and behavior.

Do not identify with your feelings. Do not say, for example, "I am sad" or "I am upset." Transpose this negativity to something else. Instead, say, "This movie made me sad" or "This job is difficult and frustrating."

Be nice to others even if you do not really want to. Is it a bad day? Behave the opposite of how you feel. Choose to spread a little optimism around you. The smiles of the people you have helped will allow you to think much more positively. Here are some suggestions to brighten the day of others:

clean the house before your spouse or roommate comes home

bring coffee or donuts to co-workers

mow your neighbor's lawn or clear their driveway in winter greet and compliment a stranger

Surround yourself with people whose company you enjoy. If you want to think positive, it is important that you are surrounded by positive people who bring out the best in you. Hang out with people who support you, are friendly, and love you the way you are.

Stop dating someone in particular because they always put you in a bad mood.

Find positive quotes or mantras. These will help you keep a positive outlook on your day. Always have them with you in your pocket and noted on a piece of paper, saving them on your phone or remembering them throughout the day.

Sign up for positive affirmation websites like those offered by Pinterest, Twitter or Facebook. These will allow you to have a social network of optimistic friends who will have a good influence on your life.

Start a diary and write it down daily. Practice turning bad into good if your days don't always end well. Make yourself a cup of coffee (or other drink you like), sit back and take the time to write in your journal. It's easy: settle in and just start writing. What good thing can you talk about? What bad memory? Don't forget anything.

Note down three things that went well and explain why Then mention three things that went wrong and also explain why

Be as specific as possible when describing these different situations.

Reread what you wrote. A given situation can seem terrible to us when we think about it in our minds. However, you may find that this is not the case that dramatic when you have read it over and over. Did you need to be so pessimistic?

Avoid negative thoughts

Identify what triggers your negative thoughts. What are the things that put you in a bad mood? And which ones make you feel guilty or make you uncomfortable? It is important that you pinpoint the triggers that plunge you into a negative emotional state. You will be better able to fight them to eliminate them permanently from your life when you have identified them.

Do you get angry or upset at the same time? Does this happen when you are faced with a particular situation? Or in the company of a certain person? What causes your anger?

Do you usually have a hard time seeing the bright side of anything? If, for example, the mere idea of being on vacation brings you no joy, it would be good to see your doctor. He can confirm whether or not you have symptoms of depression.

Surround yourself only with people who support you. Stay away from those who do not contribute to your mental well-being. Those that stress you criticize you or depress you are wasting your time and energy. Avoid them or set limits not to exceed them.

If you absolutely have to hang out with someone who always turns you on their head, or if it is impossible for you to cut off contact with someone, do everything you can to set limits. Be honest with them and let them know that you need time for yourself and that you would rather be alone.

Give less importance to what others say. If something gives you a sense of well-being, take advantage of it. On the other hand, if other things leave you completely indifferent, don't be influenced by the opinions of those around you. Listen to your inner voice and don't give too much importance to other people's opinions about yourself or your business.

Do not seek the advice of others, unless you really need it. It doesn't matter if your colleague doesn't like the name you have chosen for your cat. What matters is that you like this name!

Don't compare yourself to others anymore. Rivalries can generate many negative People. Avoid situations that force you to confront yourself to others or to compare your skills to those of others. These kinds of circumstances can lead to stress, resentment, and anxiety. So if you want to keep a positive frame of mind, avoid all situations where you will be forced to compare yourself with others or compete with them.

Stay busy. Work had and have a lot of fun. Fill in your activity schedule. That sway, you will be too busy to entertain negative thoughts. Stay focused on your activities and be productive. This will keep you from going back to your negative thoughts. Focus only on what you do and what you accomplish.

Some people like to be busy coping with negative thoughts. However, other people become negative if they have too much to do. The latter need to rest more than the others. If this is your case, allow enough break time in your schedule

Don't do a whole mountain for unimportant things. What matters is that you are happy and satisfied with your lot in life and that you can spend time with family and friends. And the rest? Put it under the category of unimportant things. Don't make it all cheese.

Block everything that annoys you on your social network. If one of your virtual friends is used to false modesty, and it bothers you, block them, and stop reading their updates. Ignore it.

If you live in a place harmful to your mental state, it would be important that you seek to improve your lifestyle to maintain an optimistic vision.

14

Cultivating Joy

Are you experiencing joy on a daily basis, or are you continually frustrated, tired, disappointed, and unhappy? I believe that if we can't appreciate what we already have, having more won't make us happy.

Wouldn't you love to have more joy in your life? It isn't something that happens to us when we're lucky; it's something that we must learn to cultivate on a daily basis.

We already have so many things to be grateful for in life, but our brain is wired to take them for granted. Have you ever been excited about a new purchase you just made? Now, how long did the excitement last before you got used to your new toy? It isn't long before you take it for granted and revert to your original level of happiness.

Let's do a simple exercise: Close your eyes and take a few seconds to think of all the things that you want in your life.

Now, what if I told you that you'd quickly take these things for granted once you get them and will focus on finding new things to acquire? That's what many people do: they spend their entire life chasing things, looking to get a bigger house, a better car, or a higher salary, yet they never feel satisfied.

There's nothing wrong with chasing things. However, you have to realize that the things you go after won't fulfill you nearly as much as you think. So, it's better to spend time appreciating all the little things you already have in your life: the security of a home, an abundance of food, your health, your friends and family, the beauty of nature that surrounds you, etc. There are so many things to be grateful for, and I'm sure you have at least a few of these things in your life.

Practicing gratitude

Gratitude, like everything else, can be cultivated. If you want to increase the amount of joy and appreciation that you experience on a daily basis, it's essential to implement a daily habit of gratitude.

There was a point in my life when I was unhappy. That's when I realized that it was my job to train my mind to help me experience more joy and gratitude. I did it by focusing on feeling more grateful for the things I already had. You can do that, too!

Below are a few things you can do to experience more profound feelings of gratitude.

Keeping a gratitude journal

Writing down what you're grateful for is a great way to train your mind to focus on the positive. Can you name three things you're thankful for right now? I bet you can. In fact, you could think of thousands.

The simple practice of writing down what you're grateful for every morning will help you experience more gratitude over time.

What about you? What are you going to write down in your gratitude journal?

Practicing gratitude meditation

Gratitude meditation is also a great way to start your day. You can find plenty of guided meditations on YouTube, but here are a few of my favorites:

- Louise Hay's Morning Meditation

- Guided Meditation on Gratitude with Deepak Chopra
- Morning Gratitude Positive Affirmations
- Morning Gratitude Affirmations - Listen for 21 Days!

Listening to uplifting music

One thing I also like to do is listen to uplifting songs in the morning. They can help you generate more positive emotions and allow you to access deep states of gratitude. I especially like this song in particular: Karen Drucker's song

Finding what works and what doesn't

We all know we should be grateful for what we have. However, knowing it doesn't help, does it? That's because being thankful is an emotion to be experienced. It's not something we can intellectualize. We have to experience it.

Feeling grateful is not easy, especially in the beginning. Repeating, "I'm grateful for X, Y, and Z" again and again doesn't mean you genuinely feel it. The key is to keep practicing and find exercises that work for you.

Maybe you like to listen to music while doing gratitude exercises. Or perhaps you prefer guided meditations. I encourage to experiment. Pick one exercise for three to four weeks, stick to it, and see how it makes you feel.

Finally, don't underestimate the power of gratitude. Imagine if you could be ecstatically happy just for being alive. We all probably should be, but we aren't. Practicing gratitude on a daily basis will allow you to feel more grateful for what you have — even if it isn't that much — and experience a decreased need for external things.

The key here is to access your emotions and not just your mind.

Blessing

Blessing things is another great way to experience more gratitude and joy in your life. You can bless virtually anything in your life. You can bless your food every time you eat, and you can bless your possessions. Interestingly enough, you can also bless seemingly adverse situations. I learned the concept of blessing things that seem unfortunate in Honore's book Prosperity for Writers. I found it so intriguing that I've started implementing it in my life.

There's also a quote that I love from Les Brown that says, "Don't say 'I'm having a bad day.' Say 'I'm having a character-building day.'"

When you have a "character-building" day, remind yourself to bless it. Our most significant breakthroughs often come after our biggest failures. You can't learn much from your successes, but you can learn a lot from your failures. The key is to accept it when we fail and consciously decide to learn from it. So, what can you bless in your life right now?

Giving more

Tony Robbins says that "the secret to living is giving" and I agree with that statement. Nowadays, we're continually trying to get more: more attention, more fame, more money, more things, or more friends. Unfortunately, this rarely leads to more happiness. If anything, it leaves us unhappy and unfulfilled.

Have you ever felt good about yourself for giving money to charity or to a cause that's dear to your heart? I believe that we're naturally wired to give. Without giving to one another, human beings would have probably died out a long time ago. The more we give to others, the better we feel about ourselves.

In fact, there's an experiment in which they gave participants money that they could spend either on themselves or others. The study showed that those who chose to spend money on others experienced more happiness than those who spent the money on themselves.

In his classic book How to Stop Worrying and Start Living, Dale Carnegie argued that if a depressed person were to spend each day focusing on what they could do for others, their depression would cease within two weeks. While this may not be true, I can say for sure that giving to others is one of the most effective ways to increase our levels of happiness.

So, how can you give more in your day-to-day life?

Tithing

Do you give away part of your income every month?

Many people recommend that we give 10% of our salary to charity, including Jim Rohn, one of my favorite personal development experts. Tithing on a regular basis helps us express our gratitude and overcome the scarcity mindset that many of us have.

Many people wish rich people would be less greedy. Well, are you unwilling to give 10% of your income, or even a smaller percentage, to charities or causes you want to support right now? If so, you probably won't want to give away part of your fortune when you get rich. After all, giving to charity has more to do with our mindset than with the amount of money we have in our bank account. Many rich and poor people are greedy. Money just magnifies people's vices and virtues.

The Bible says "Give, and you shall receive," which could be accurate. What we can say is that the more you give away money, the more open you become to receiving it. The more you do for others, the more open you are to their reciprocation.

It goes both ways. The more you do something for yourself, the more you can encourage others to do the same. Let's say you're trying to sell a product that costs a few hundred dollars and you're prospecting new clients. If you've never invested a few hundred dollars in a product yourself, it'll be difficult to convince potential customers to buy your product. However, when you regularly purchase and benefit from products with a similar cost, it suddenly becomes less challenging. You start believing that your product isn't that expensive, and it will show in your body language, facial expression, vocal tone, and emotional state.

This goes to show that being at peace with money, or anything else you want to attract in your life, will allow you to attract more of it.

The bottom-line is that experiencing more joy and gratitude in your life is an inside job. You have to decide that you're going to be happier. It starts by conditioning your mind every single day. That's why I like to start my day with meditation, stretching, listening to uplifting songs, and then reading old entries from my gratitude journal. Now, I wake up happier in the morning. That's an automatic response based on the conditioning of my mind. You can do the same.

15

Positive Thinking is the Key to Success

It keeps tension at bay

When something terrible happens in your life, you get bombarded with negative thoughts. It can happen for personal or work-related reasons. In some cases, it affects certain parts of your life. Belief in positivity could help you escape stress. The trick is learning about what's happened. To move on as weight is the key to success can only become a hindrance to your development.

You are living a happy and healthy life

People with a high-stress level appear to have some physical and psychological disorders. Weight loss, anxiety, and sleep disturbances are typical among people under stress. Positive thought helps you that all of that. If you are doing the best quality in any situation, you will achieve the best physical and mental health.

It boosts your trust and self-esteem

If you are sure of your skills, you win half the fight. Positive power fosters faith. It increases your self-esteem when you work and believe in your skills independently. The critical prerequisite for you to remain inspired in life is positive thinking.

You should make good choices

Lots of people regret their decisions during the stressful phases of life. Tension or stress holds the cognitive ability down. It makes you rush to make a decision. On the other hand, decision making should be simple for a rational thinker. He or she should give the actual scenario the right amount of consideration. To a good thinker, it's the secret to success.

It will lead you to success

The power of positivity will help you discover your skills. Through an optimistic outlook, you will find the ray of light in the darkest of hours. Both of these are the key to achieving success. Optimism makes you feel happiness, too. It makes your personality appealing to the men. This way, you can help other people improve their way of thinking. You can learn a lot from them too.

Positive Thinking and Actions

Knew you that constructive thinking is one of the most important keys to success?

With this element, achieving success, improving relationships, getting better health, and enjoying happiness, fulfillment, and inner peace is easier. This key also helps to make things run more smoothly and with less tension in the everyday affairs of life. An optimistic outlook makes life happier and more exciting.

This key also requires you to take constructive action, as outcomes require positive thinking as well as affirmative action.

Positive affirmation is contagious.

People choose the mental moods around you and accordingly. Think of happiness, good health, and achievement, and you're going to make people admire you and want to help you because they love the vibrations that a positive mind emitted.

Effective positive thinking

Produces results are far more than merely saying a few encouraging phrases, or reminding yourself that everything will be perfect. Your mental disposition will predominate. It's not enough for a couple of moments to think positively, and then let doubts and lack of confidence invade your mind. It takes some time and some inner work.

You're Secret to Success Tips

1. Only use encouraging words when you think and speak. Using terms like, "I can", "it is possible," etc.
2. Enable to your consciousness only feelings of joy, power, and achievement.
3. Disregard negative feelings, and forget them. Refuse to think about these emotions, replacing them with positive, pleasant feelings.
4. Using words and mental images of energy, happiness, and success in your conversation.
5. Until beginning with some plan of action, imagine the positive result clearly in your mind. When you imagine the effects of focus and conviction, you'll be shocked.
6. Read at least one page of an inspirational book every day.
7. Watch movies that will make you feel happy.
8. Minimize the time listening to the radio and reading the newspapers.
9. Associate yourself with people who have good feelings.

10. Just sit up straight with your back and walk. That will boost your faith and inner power.
11. Talk, swim, or do some other physical activity. Which helps the production of a more positive attitude.

Stay positive and expect only positive outcomes and conditions, even though the present circumstances are not the way you want them. Your mental disposition will, in time, influence, and change your outer life and circumstances accordingly.

Why You Need A Positive Attitude And How To Gain It?

Adopting a positive outlook as a way of life will help you deal with your daily life affairs more quickly, and will bring meaningful changes to your life. A good outlook will make you an optimist, which will help you escape concerns which negative thinking.

Developing this mentality will make you a happier person who sees life's bright side and wants the best. It is also a state of mind worth cultivating.

What's a Great Attitude?

Here are a few definitions which try to explain what a positive attitude is and how it manifests itself.

1. This is a mental condition that hopes to happen as best as possible. This is the practice of believing that things will turn well and not allowing negative thoughts and suspicions to interrupt this confidence, simply, positive thinking.
2. It is critical thinking-you think and believes you can find solutions. This means being involved in addressing problems. It's not enough to believe things' going to work out all right. You will need to think critically about and execute positive approaches.

3. Its innovative thinking-looking through a wider perspective at life and problems, and seeking new solutions. You're not afraid to look for new ways of doing things with a good attitude. It makes you special and more able to help you do more than anyone.

4. Optimism-It is one of its main features. This means that there is hope and anticipation that things will change, and the plans will work out well.

5. Motivation-It is the desire and zest for doing things and attaining goals. You are keen on performing, investing energy and time on research, studies, or reaching a goal when there is motivation present. You are empowered when you are sure of yourself, believe in your abilities, and let nothing stop you.

6. Happiness-Typically, a person with a positive attitude, is happy and content.

In many ways and in many circumstances, a positive mind-frame will benefit you. This will help you stay calm in tough times, not lose hope, and, despite challenges or defeats, continue everything you do.

How do you know you've got a good attitude?

1. Figure out if you have the following habits: Do you intend your acts to produce a positive result?

2. Would you inspire yourself and others, and promote them?

3. Not giving up when facing challenges and having problems and not feeling down.

4. You look at loss and difficulties as veiled blessings. You are learning from them, and you are not repeating them.

5. You believe in yourself and your skills and competences.

6. Would you believe you possess adequate self-esteem and self-confidence to manage the affairs of your everyday life with confidence?

7. One of the key characteristics of a healthy mind frame is the ability to remain resilient to negative thoughts, negative words, negative people, and discouragement and not allow them to influence your mental state.
8. Look for ideas rather than focusing on issues?
9. In this state of mind, you are curious and open-minded and are thus able to consider and seek to pursue possibilities.

A positive mindset leads to success and satisfaction and can change your entire life. Look at the bright side of life, and it fills the whole life with light. Not only does this light affect you and how you look at the world, but it also impacts the atmosphere and the people around you.

It is infectious if the mindset is high enough. It's like you're radiating light around you.

This is one of the reasons why creative visualization is important for performance, contentment, and happiness.

The Benefits of a Positive Attitude

- I have already listed many of the advantages and value of maintaining a positive attitude. A little clarity will also make it even simpler.
- It helps you accomplish goals and achieve success.
- It can bring greater joy to your life.
- It makes you an enjoyable person to be with and makes it easier to be liked and to have friends.
- It creates more energy, anticipation, interest, and even curiosity, making life more interesting.
- Positive attitude increases the willingness to trust and gives optimism and anticipation for a better future.
- In carrying out assignments and focusing on goals, it increases your motivation, and you can encourage and motivate others too.

- Obstacles and challenges do not ruin your joy and satisfaction. You are not focused on them, and you are focusing on the solutions.
- The mentality of one is infectious and influences others. Customers will like you when it's nice and friendly and want your company.
- Life smiles at you when you feel good and happy and expect good things to happen.

Negative mentality says: You can't succeed.

A positive mindset says: You will succeed.

When you showed a pessimistic disposition and were predicting disappointment and difficulties, now is the time to change the way you think. Now it is the time to get rid of negative thoughts and behavior and continue to live a happier life of hope, motivation, and zest. When you've tried and failed to do so in the past, that just means you haven't done yet and should try again.

When your ego insists that you can't fix it, then don't listen. Progress is not going to happen immediately, but it will happen with a little perseverance.

Easy Tips to Develop a Healthy Attitude:

1. Choose happily. Yeah, this is an optional matter. When negative feelings come into your mind, just refuse to look at it and worry about it. Do whatever you can to replace them with positive feelings.
2. Look on life's other side. It is a question of preference and repeated attempts. There's still some positive in it, some wisdom and lessons to learn, no matter how difficult a situation is.
3. Select to be positive. Like to believe things improve for the better.

4. Find more opportunities to smile. If you look around you, you will find these explanations. There are humorous things, amusing accidents, nice things and small successes in everyday life. All of them are a smile to reason.

5. Have faith in yourself, and believe the world will help. Clear confidence in yourself and willingness to deal with any situation fosters a positive outlook within you.

6. Associate with happy people, as joy is infectious.

7. Write inspirational stories about inspiring people, whether happy or miserable. Don't envy or jealously envy them. Only learn from their stories, and let them encourage you to do similar things and empower you.

8. Write quotes which are motivational. These quotes can be found on the Web and in our quotes list. I recommend you read a few in the morning, before going to work, and in the evening, before going to bed.

9. To inspire and empower you, repeat the affirmations.

10. Visualize in your life just what you want to happen, and stop contemplating and visualizing what you don't want.

11. Learn how to grow a calm mind and master your thoughts. If you can concentrate, you can more easily turn your mind to the thoughts you like, and stop negative thoughts.

16

Enjoy Your Life

Living your best life and being your best self is more than just accomplishing all of your goals. It's also important that you are able to enjoy your life. After all, what's the point if you aren't even happy? There are a few ways that you can help yourself to enjoy your life. It'll make your goals all seem worth it. You'll be able to be more positive and have a greater appreciation for life. Enjoying your life will allow you to see more clearly what matters to you and what life is all about. You'll feel free and creative. Of course, you can live your life and hate every moment of it. You can suffer through every day, not liking your life and wishing things were different. Or, you can actually take steps to make your life enjoyable for you so that you can make the most of it. Practicing gratitude can help you to truly appreciate all that life offers, and you may feel more positive as a result. Appreciating yourself, those around you, and everything that you encounter can give you some positivity. You may also learn how to focus on the present moment, as that will allow you to experience the greatest joy. You will live in the moment instead of dwelling on what happened in the past or what might happen in the future. Learning to do what you love can really help you to be successful and happy. Often, we think that we can only choose one of these, yet it's important to remember that you can have it all. Finally, you'll learn about how and why to constantly improve yourself. If you remain the same, nothing will happen and you won't experience growth. Enjoying your life also requires you to enjoy change.

Practicing Gratitude

Taking a bit of time every day to practice gratitude can highly benefit you. It's super important to be able to be grateful, thankful, and appreciative of all that life offers. When you practice gratitude, it's hard not to be a positive person. You'll be able to focus on everything that you have instead of everything that you want, which can have a huge impact on you. It'll be easier to find the positive traits of people in your life and to find positivity in everything that happens.

It's quite simple to practice gratitude. It's free, quick, and can even be fun. Just a few minutes a day can make a huge difference, and there are many ways to practice gratitude. You'll be a much more positive person for doing so, you'll feel better about your life, and you'll be much more motivated as well. Additionally, you may choose; however, you would like to practice gratitude. Because there are so many ways to do so, you may switch it up every day. You have many options to choose from, so there must be at least one that works for you.

You may keep a gratitude journal for yourself that you write in every day. You may have a gratitude list that you add to every day. This may even just be a portion of your journal. Simply writing down five things that you are grateful for each day can really help you to focus on what you love. This is great for the morning, as you can start your day on a positive note. You may also want to consider doing this before you go to bed so that you end the day thinking about what you were grateful for throughout the day. This can leave a better feeling about the day as a whole.

There is so much to appreciate! While outside, notice the beauty of the sky, plants, animals, and nature as a whole. Remember to appreciate your friends. They're the ones that are there for you and that you spend time with. The same is true for family. Before eating, take a small moment to be grateful for the food you have; not everyone gets a choice. Find the good in everything. Pause throughout the day and remember how great life is.

Express your gratitude. Tell others how much you love and appreciate them. Smile more often, especially at strangers; they're people too! Practice random acts of kindness without expecting anything in return. Call up friends and family just to say hello. Volunteer for causes that you're passionate about. Compliment others. Contact those who you haven't talked to in a while. Even spending time with others is a great way to express gratitude. Remember to appreciate the time you have with them. Thank those that serve you in your life. This could be a cashier, a janitor, or a flight attendant. These people are essential to the economy, yet they are rarely thanked for their work. You might make someone's day much better for it. Remember to express gratitude towards yourself. Be grateful for both your strengths and weaknesses, and remember to be grateful that you are alive.

It's also important to appreciate the challenges of life. It can be fairly easy to name all of the positive aspects of life that you're grateful for. However, it's important to also remember to express gratitude for challenges and mistakes. They make you who you are.

Focusing on the Present Moment

Practicing mindfulness and living in the present moment can really help you to enjoy your life more. You'll have a greater appreciation for what's happening now instead of focusing on what already happened or what might happen. This can really help you to ease your stress and anxiety, and you'll be much more aware of what's happening. It will also allow you to develop a greater appreciation for life, as you will be fully present in the moment.

Focusing on the present can help you to appreciate others more. During conversations, it's common to simply wait for your turn to talk. Instead of fully listening to what the other person is saying, you plan out in your head what you're going to say while only listening to about half of what the other person is saying. It will make a huge difference. Others will really appreciate you for doing so, and you may form better relationships with them. You may even inspire others to listen better in their conversations. You may also appreciate others more because you are there with them fully. This can allow you to really enjoy the moment instead of being worried about other things.

Being present can help you to stop being so worried about everything. You'll be able to focus on the past. Being present will stop you from thinking about everything that went wrong in the past, any mistakes that you (or others) made, and any grudges you hold. You'll stop worrying about what might happen in the future. The reality is, you can't predict the future, as nothing ever goes completely to plan. It's best to appreciate the present for what it is, and life will be so much for enjoyable as a result.

You may be more present by directing your thoughts towards the present. When you sense yourself drifting, bring yourself back to reality. You may try to focus on something that's happening. Perhaps you prefer to focus on your senses. Meditation can really help you to get your mind in the present. You'll be able to focus much better on what's going on now. Gratitude can also help you to focus on the present. You may think of what you are grateful for now, and that will allow you to pay attention to that and really appreciate it.

Living in the present moment can also help you to appreciate what you have instead of what you want. We're never done. Your to-do list will never be empty. There will always be new things to buy. Change is always happening. If you can live in the present instead of focusing on everything else that's happening, you'll feel so much better. It will help you to appreciate what you have right now. You can stop thinking about how life used to be and how it was better then. You can stop thinking that you'll be happy once something else happens. Appreciate life for what it is right now, not later.

Doing What You Love

Your life should be filled with love, joy, and happiness. We often try to force ourselves to continue with things that we don't like. We do what we think we should be doing, or we follow the path of others. However, this won't get you anywhere. You must follow yourself, as you'll be there everywhere you go. Learn to spend your time doing what you love, not what others love.

Eliminate what you don't like from your routine. This can make a huge impact on you, and you'll be much happier. Everything can be changed. Perhaps you don't like going to the gym, and it really doesn't suit you, but you feel like you have to because you want to exercise and stay in shape. There are so many other options. You can run, bike, swim, join a fitness class, or even work out from home. Think about your daily routine and anything that you don't particularly like. How can you change it to be more enjoyable? There are many ways that you can make your day better, and this is a simple solution for you.

Do something every day that you love. Every day, take some time to do something that you love. This could be as little as spending a few minutes reading a book from a genre (or about a subject) that you enjoy. Make a list of what you love, and commit to doing at least one of those things every day. It doesn't have to be something that lasts for hours, costs money, or requires you to go anywhere special. It should just be something that brings you joy. When you take time to yourself, you will also see your worth and how great it feels to take care of yourself.

Make changes if you aren't happy with where you are. If you don't like your job, find a new one. Even if you are making good money, you can make money doing anything as long as you're passionate about it. Nothing should hold you back. There's no reason to spend your time doing something that you don't enjoy when there is so much more to life. If you want to move, do it. If there's something you want to buy, save up for it. If not now, when? Don't keep delaying your happiness.

Discover more about yourself and what you like. Every day, try something new. This could be trying new food, going somewhere different, or exploring a new subject. You won't know if you like it until you try it. You may automatically assume that you don't like everything that you haven't tried. Even if you don't like it, now you know that you don't like it. Yet, you may discover many new things that you never would have imagined that you like. Perhaps you order the same thing on the menu each time you go to a restaurant because it's your "favorite item on the menu." Yet, you don't know if it truly is your favorite until you've had everything on the menu. You may try something new and have that be your new favorite. It's an automatic no if you never even try.

17

Conclusion

You are now aware of how life and stress can affect your mind, as well as how anxiety, depression, and anger can affect you. These are all important to properly deal with. Once you do, you'll feel so much better. Practicing self-discipline is also important, and you can practice controlling your thoughts so that you can make better decisions in your daily life. You may work on your attitude, which can help you to think much more clearly about what you want. Plus, you'll be much more motivated to accomplish your goals. Eliminating negative attitudes and replacing them with positives ones can help you to feel better and improve your relationship with others as well. You may now focus on what you want by setting goals for yourself. You've learned about the types of goals that you can set, how to figure out which goals to set, setting your priorities, and planning out your goals. These are all great steps to take so that you can find out what you really want in life. Time management is a great skill for you to practice. It's great to start planning out your day, setting daily goals, prioritizing your goals, and maximizing your time while avoiding wasted time.

You can start changing your habits. This will require you to identify bad habits that you have, implement good habits to replace them, stay committed to your habits, and avoid making common habit mistakes. Meditation is a great skill for you to learn. You learned about what it is, how to do it, the benefits of it, and how to spice it up. With this knowledge, you can start meditating and improving your life by doing so. You may also begin to enjoy your life even more. This is possible by practicing gratitude, focusing on the present moment, doing what you love, and constantly improving yourself. Doing all of these can help you to enjoy your life more. It's also possible to become a better person. This can be accomplished by adding more kindness and compassion into your life, practicing patience, learning to understand both yourself and others, and avoiding overreacting. Finally, you can defeat your obsessiveness. After identifying if you are obsessive, you learned how to stop and how to stop worrying so much about perfectionism. Everything you learned will take some practice.

It's time for you to define what success means to you and start on your path to reach it. Keep in mind that your vision of success might be different than the traditional definition. In fact, success will look different to every person. Think carefully and decide what you want your long-term goals to be. Maybe it's to open a business, or write a novel, or make enough money to keep your family comfortable or to start a charity for a cause you care about. It can be any number of things, as long as it's something that speaks to you and that will continue to motivate you on the difficult journey ahead. It can even be something vaguer, such as happiness, as long as you can break it down into smaller goals that are achievable. Whatever it is, write it down. Start breaking it down into smaller goals that will lead to your success and even smaller daily goals that will guarantee you'll have something to celebrate every day. Then, begin to cultivate your habits. Use the techniques throughout this book to change your habits and your mindset. Remember that it will be difficult, as our brains are naturally resistant to change. Keep your ultimate goal in mind as your motivation, and make your changes gradually, starting with exercise.

You may be wondering, like most of us do, what happens after you've reached your goals and achieved your success? First of all, take a step back and admire all you've done to reach that point. It can be easy to get caught up in the day-to-day work that goes with your success and forget to acknowledge that you've reached your goals. It's important to care about the journey but don't forget to check in from time to time to see where you are. Remember the little celebrations you had for your small wins? Now, you get to have a full-blown celebration. Throw a party, take a spa day, or whatever feels like a big reward to you. You deserve it. Plan this out in advance and make it part of your dream board, because then you will know for sure, deep down in your gut, that you are here, that you made it.

After you celebrate, it's time to redefine your success, so that you don't get stuck with no idea where to go next. Success must be a constantly evolving thing. This will keep you from getting burnt out, and keep your mind working towards the next thing, as well as keep you from getting caught up in every little detail that differs between the reality of your success and how you imagine it would be. Maintain your brain plasticity and keep up with your habits just as before, as these are not something you reach an end goal for. They are continuous, and having them to build your day around will help you not to worry as much about the future, because the future likely looks a lot like today does, with your habits filling up much of the time. Your next goals will be easier to reach with the foundation you've built for yourself, with all the resources you have acquired and relationships you have built. If you love what you're currently doing, then your new goal could be to maintain that. Build in redundancies to protect it and start finding ways to refine it even more. It will still require hard work and dedication to flex around the changing world, so keep abreast of what's going on around you and make sure you can adapt with the times. Or, look to the next level of your current position, what you can do to further your successes and reach out. For example, if you started that charity and it's a huge success locally, look at taking it statewide and having other branches. If your local restaurant took off and maintaining that doesn't sound interesting enough, consider opening up another location, or taking it on the road in a food truck, or getting your recipes onto grocery store shelves. There's no shame in staying put if you like where you're at, but the potential to expand is limited only by your imagination.

It can be tempting to fall into a negative mindset once you've reached your big goals, simply because you might not feel all that different. By this point, your habits should be ingrained, but you may feel the desire to stop putting effort towards bettering yourself. It's okay to take a break while you celebrate your success but get back to your healthy ways as soon as possible. Your mind and health can decay without proper maintenance, and this could cause you to slide backward from your success. You can also lose the routine feeling to your hard-won habits if you break from them long enough, meaning you'll have to work to get them ingrained all over again! It's also possible to be overwhelmed by all that you're doing, especially if you're dealing with a lot of change. Don't forget to utilize your support system, and delegate tasks to others. There is also the fear that you'll lose your hard-won success, the feeling that what you've achieved isn't stable and can be taken away from you. As we discussed earlier, our minds aren't built for satisfaction, and we have to live and work at that frequency. Remind yourself that you reached your goals through your own hard work and merit, and that can't be taken away from you, no matter what happens to your business in a year, in five years, or fifty. Your success is yours.

Your definition of success may change along the way. That's okay. Check in with yourself frequently, and adjust your long-term goals as needed. There is no shame in redirecting, as we are human and our feelings about things change constantly. Your motivation depends on your emotions, so it's important that you keep your goals in line with what you feel and believe. As you gain new information and make changes to your life, you may desire different things for your success, or find yourself with new opinions or values that aren't in line with your original pursuits. Ultimately, you should look for happiness in your life. That is real success. Your success should contribute to your happiness in a major way, and vice versa, and if they aren't then something has gone wrong along the way. Keep in mind that this does not mean you have to be successful before you can be happy – if you're currently unhappy, you need to make immediate changes rather than waiting for a "big break."

Happiness and success are two separate things, and though they can be related, one doesn't instantly bring about the other. Ingrid Bergman said, "Success is getting what you want; happiness is wanting what you get." You'll need to put in the work to make sure those things match up. But there is plenty that you can do to earn happiness, right here and now, while you wait for your diligent work to pay off and get you to your dreams. A lot of these habits we've talked about, like exercise and reading and improving relationships, these activities make your every-day better and brighter and full of life. What you train yourself to spend your time on can bring you happiness right now, and this is what we mean by enjoying the journey. The dream board version of your end goal can be far off in the future, but your everyday life is now. Make every moment a win.

Are you ready to live a happy and successful life full of wealth and abundance? If so, make this guide your best friend and heed the recommendations that have been outlined herein. Success is not implausible. Forget about what people have told you before. Starting today, you can change your habits and start on the journey that leads you to a complete transformation.

Sometimes, when you're going through a rough patch, it might be challenging to be grateful, I know. But believe me, there is always something to be grateful for, such as you, your body, your talents, your friends, your family, or nature. Start small. When I was jobless, I was grateful for drinking a coffee in the sun, having a good night's sleep, and having friends. Instead of starting your day by complaining about what you don't have or by dreading what is to come, start it by saying thank you for what you have. Focus on everything that's going well for you.

18

Letras Itinerantes

10% of the sale of this book is destined for "Fundación Letras Itinerantes", dedicated to promoting reading in Mayan communities, preserving the language and providing quality education in Quintana Roo, Mexico.

CPSIA information can be obtained
at www.ICGtesting.com
Printed in the USA
LVHW080313300121
677805LV00008B/403